AF600519

REVERENTIAL FEAR IN MATRIMONIAL CASES IN ASIATIC COUNTRIES: ROTA CASES

THE CATHOLIC UNIVERSITY OF AMERICA
CANON LAW STUDIES
No. 294

Reverential Fear in Matrimonial Cases in Asiatic Countries: Rota Cases

A HISTORICAL SYNOPSIS AND A COMMENTARY

BY

REV. ROCH F. KNOPKE, O.F.M., M.A., J.C.L.
PRIEST OF THE PROVINCE OF THE MOST HOLY NAME OF JESUS

A DISSERTATION

SUBMITTED TO THE FACULTY OF THE SCHOOL OF CANON LAW OF THE CATHOLIC UNIVERSITY OF AMERICA IN PARTIAL FULFILLMENT OF THE REQUIREMENTS FOR THE DEGREE OF DOCTOR OF CANON LAW

THE CATHOLIC UNIVERSITY OF AMERICA PRESS
WASHINGTON, D. C.
1949

IMPRIMI POTEST:
THOMAS PLASSMANN, O.F.M., S.T.D
Minister Provincialis

NIHIL OBSTAT:
LUDOVICUS H. MOTRY, S.T.D., J.C.D.
Censor Deputatus

IMPRIMATUR:
✠ PATRITIUS A. O'BOYLE, D.D.
Archiepiscopus Washingtoniensis

Washingtoniensis, die 24 augusti, 1949.

Printed in the United States of America
by
THE ACADEMY PRESS
WASHINGTON 14, D. C.

MARIAE
REGINAE MISSIONUM

Table of Contents

Foreword

The contract of marriage, raised by our Lord, Jesus Christ, to the dignity of the sacrament of matrimony, demands a constant and vigilant care on the part of the Church for the protection of its contractual and sacramental elements. This the Church accomplishes in its courts, through its legislation and by means of its decrees. In its gradual spread over the entire earth the Church has met many civilizations and diversified cultures. Herein lay a great need for the adjusting of its laws in non-essentials that could be waived, and for insistence upon its laws in essentials that had to be maintained.

In China, and in the nations influenced by its culture, marriage has been held in high esteem. Great powers have accrued to the parents for the purpose of arranging the marriages of their children, so that the best interests of the family and the clan might be served. Such powers if well used served their purpose admirably; if misused they came in conflict with a fundamental demand of the legislation of the Church, namely, that the parties entering marriage make their contract with a free consent. To examine this conflict is the purpose of this dissertation.

In an appendix at the end of this work there is furnished a chronological arrangement of all the Rota cases cited.

Special thanks are due to The John Day Company, Inc., for permission to quote from Lin Yutang's *My Country and My People,* and to E. P. Dutton and Company, Inc., for permission to quote from Shiao-Tung Fei's *Peasant Life in China.*

The writer wishes to express his thanks, due to so many who aided him on so many counts, for the assistance and encouragement that have helped to bring this work to its conclusion.

Part One—Historical Synopsis

CHAPTER I

FUNDAMENTAL NOTIONS

In order to establish the meaning of reverential fear, the concepts of force and fear will have to be examined. The two terms, force and fear, are closely connected, so much so that one is sometimes used for the other, or both are used together, since an action resulting from them has the element of lack of volition in the passive subject of the force or fear.

Article 1. Force

Force is an impetus of a degree greater than can be resisted.[1] Various terms are used, but they have this meaning in common, that the passive subject is operated upon against its inclination. In modern works, the terms violence, force, and coercion are used indiscriminately to a great extent.[2] The fundamental and necessary distinction of force, quite generally accepted, is into absolute and moral force. Absolute force (also known as physical force) in the strict sense is that which cannot be resisted in any way whatsoever. To apply the concept to man as a rational being, it may be defined as an impetus, exerted on external acts by an extrinsic cause, which impetus cannot be resisted, and which the passive subject undergoes without any consent to the external act produced.[3]

Moral force (also known as conditional or causative force) is that which could be resisted, at least partially. Under the concept of moral force some authors include also that force which a passive

---

[1] D. (4, 2) 2—Paulus' definition. The translations are the writer's whenever no other indication is given.

[2] Juarez, *De Impedimento Matrimoniali Vis et Metus* (Murciae, Typis Sancti Francisci, 1928), p. 3 (hereafter cited *Vis et Metus*).

[3] Cf. Juarez, *Vis et Metus,* p. 3.

subject cannot resist, but in the execution of which he is not at the same time an unwilling subject.[4]

Coronata gives a different analysis of absolute and moral force. He claims that they are specifically different, and that moral force cannot be considered a species of force as defined by Paulus. If moral (causative) force is defined as the impetus of an imminent evil which can be absolutely resisted, it should be considered as causing fear, and from this viewpoint moral force is only another aspect of fear, i. e., moral force is the cause, fear, the result.[5]

Hence, acts performed under the influence of this moral force are *voluntaria* and *involuntaria secundum quid.* There is present a true internal consent of a free will, although *secundum quid* the liberty of consent is lessened.[6]

Obviously, absolute force precludes all consent, and matrimonial consent can not be given when such force is operative. Under the influence of moral force some consent can be present. Accordingly one must still find an answer for the question regarding the circumstances under which such a force does preclude a valid marriage consent. It is to be noted that force is a cause operating on a passive subject. The effect of this cause is fear. It is fear arising from the moral force that impels the passive subject to act. Hence force and fear are correlative terms, in the relation of cause and effect. With this distinction in mind, one finds no difficulty in the occasional indiscriminate use of these terms as found in canonical discussions.[7]

---

[4] Cf. Cappello, *Tractatus Canonico-Moralis de Sacramentis* (3 vols. in 6, Vol. III, parts 1 and 2, *De Matrimonio,* 4. ed., Romae: Marietti, 1939), III, n. 605, 2 (Vol. III hereafter cited *De Matrimonio*).

[5] Coronata, *Institutiones Iuris Canonici, De Sacramentis* (3 vols., Taurini: Marietti, 1943-1946), III, n. 467 (Vol. III hereafter cited *De Matrimonio*); Coronata, *Institutiones Iuris Canonici* (2. ed., 5 vols., Taurini: Marietti, 1939-1947), I, n. 149 (p. 179, note 1) (hereafter cited *Institutiones*).

[6] Wernz, *Ius Decretalium* (3. ed. 6 vols. in 10, Prati, 1913-1915), Vol. IV, *Ius Matrimoniale,* n. 261 (hereafter cited *Ius Matrimoniale*); Coronata, *De Matrimonio,* n. 467.

[7] Wernz, *Ius Matrimoniale,* n. 261; Coronata, *Institutiones,* I, n. 150 (p. 179, note 9).

ARTICLE 2. FEAR

Fear is defined as a mental perturbation caused by an imminent or future danger.[8] It is conceivably possible that the mind could calmly weigh the circumstances of an impending evil, and then decide on a course of action motivated by prudence, so that the emotions would in no way be influenced by the specter of fear. It seems better, then, to consider the "mental perturbation" as primarily relating to the mind, though it accidentally can, and usually does, affect the emotions.[9] In view, then, of this usual double effect which accompanies the "mental perturbation", it seems fully warranted to regard the latter as affecting mind and emotions alike.[10]

Fear is distinguished not only in its cause, but also in its manner and intensity. In its cause the fear may derive either from an intrinsic or from an extrinsic agency. Logically, fear *ab extrinseco* results from any extrinsic cause, whether it be a free agent (as man), or a necessary agent (as shipwreck), and fear *ab intrinseco* results from an internal and necessary cause (as sickness).[11] According to the tenor of the Code, however, there is better warrant to consider intrinsic fear as that which results from a necessary cause, whether internal or external to the individual, and extrinsic fear as that which is caused by a free human agent.[12] Either distinction may be accepted, since both the purely intrinsic fear and also the extrinsic fear which derives from a necessary cause are practically of the same import in moral matters.[13]

---

[8] D. (4, 2) 1.

[9] Cf. Sangmeister, *Force and Fear as Precluding Matrimonial Consent,* The Catholic University of America Canon Law Studies, n. 80 (Washington, D. C.: The Catholic University of America, 1932), p. 7 (hereafter cited *Force and Fear*).

[10] Claeys Bouuaert, "De metus influxu quoad valorem actuum et quoad delicta et poenas secundum Codicem Iuris Canonici"—*Ius Pontificium* (Romae, 1921-1940), VI (1926), 105-106 (hereafter cited "De metus influxu").

[11] Wernz, *Ius Matrimoniale,* n. 261.

[12] Sanchez, *Disputationum de Sancto Matrimonii Sacramento Libri Tres* (3 vols. in 1, Antwerpiae, 1626), Lib. IV, disp. XII, n. 2 (hereafter cited *De Matrimonii Sacramento*).

[13] Sangmeister, *Force and Fear,* p. 8, note 15.

In its manner the effected fear may be just or unjust. If the effected fear is to be just, the inflicting agent must not only have the strict right to inflict it, but he must also inflict it in a lawful manner. Otherwise the fear is unjust.

In its intensity the effected fear may be complete, grave, or slight. Complete fear is that which overthrows the use of reason (*perturbans usum rationis*). Grave fear is that which results from a threatened grave evil which can be avoided only with great difficulty. If the threatened evil is not grave, or if it can be avoided without great difficulty, the fear is called slight.

Grave fear is subdivided into absolute and relative fear. It is absolute if the threatened evil is objectively grave. It is relative if the threatened evil is slight in itself, but grave in relation to the one who sustains the fear, as in the case of children, of the timid, of those leading sheltered lives, etc. For this reason absolutely and relatively grave fear are considered equivalent whenever there is question of the voluntariness and validity of a human act.[14]

A further distinction, not always mentioned by authors at this point, may be made between antecedent and concomitant fear, or, as the Latin phrase has it, *operari ex metu, vel cum metu.* When one acts *from* fear, the fear is the cause of the act, and is considered antecedent. When one acts *with* fear, the fear does not move the subject to act, and hence the fear is only concomitant. In the case of concomitant fear it may well happen that the will is not only not restrained, but also that the intrinsic impulse of the *voluntarium* is greatly augmented. Such was the case in the Passion of Christ, and in the sufferings of the martyrs.[15] On the contrary, antecedent fear moves the apostate to apostatize in the face of suffering and death.[16]

Article 3. Reverential Fear

At this point many authors bring in the question of reverential fear, but dismiss it by saying that in itself it is not sufficient to

---

[14] Sangmeister, *Force and Fear,* pp. 9-10; Wernz, *Ius Matrimoniale,* n. 261.

[15] Frins, *De Actibus Humanis* (2. ed., 2 vols., Friburgi Brisgoviae, 1897), I, n. 284; Merkelbach, *Summa Theologiae Moralis* (3. ed., 3 vols., Parisiis: Desclee̓, 1939), Vol. I, n. 72, 3°.

[16] Sangmeister, *Force and Fear,* p. 10; cf. also *Sacrae Romanae Rotae Decisiones seu Sententiae quae prodierunt ab anno 1909* (Romae, 1912—), XXIX (1937), 355 (hereafter cited *Decisiones*).

invalidate marriage,[17] or declare that it is to be judged according to the principles which obtain with regard to fear as affecting the act of religious profession or the reception of sacred Orders. According to this latter doctrine the same principles find a proportionate application, *ceteris paribus,* in the case of fear as affecting the act of contracting marriage.[18]

In the discussion of reverential fear it will be necessary to examine more closely the nature of reverential fear and the effect it may have on the giving of matrimonial consent. Reverential fear may be defined as "a descrying or discerning of a future evil as coming to us from those under whose lawful power we live and in whose regard we sense a duty of homage and respect."[19] In consequence of this acknowledged duty of homage and respect, the inferior will experience a sense of shame in not obeying the will of his superior. An act thus influenced would be prompted by the consideration of reverence due the superior. Such a prompting is usually accompanied with the fear that through non-compliance one would reap the indignation of the superior. An act thus performed would be prompted by the consideration of reverential fear.[20]

It remains to analyse the nature of this fear. Perhaps it can be treated comprehensively under the categories of a mere reverential fear and a qualified reverential fear. *Mere* reverential fear is that by which one fears the indignation of another under whose power one lives.[21]

The definition as just given is phrased with a view to eliminating from consideration that type of fear which in a normal person could preclude a true matrimonial consent. Hence *mere* reverential fear as defined will always be considered as in the category of slight fear, and as never inherently precluding the possibility of a true matrimonial consent. In this connection it is necessary to

---

17 Wernz, *Ius Matrimoniale,* n. 261.

18 Ferraris, *Prompta Bibliotheca Canonica, Iuridica, Moralis, Theologica, necnon Ascetica, Polemica, Rubricistica, Historica* (9 vols., Romae, 1885-1899), s. v. *Metus,* n. 24.

19 Pontius, *De Sacramento Matrimonii* (2. ed., Bruxellis, 1627), Lib. IV, cap. 5, n. 1—quoted by *Decisiones,* XXIX (1937), 86.

20 Cf. Pontius, *De Sacramento Matrimonii,* Lib. IV, cap. 5, nn. 1 & 2.

21 *Decisiones,* XXVIII (1936), 705.

advert to the fact that parents have the right to oppose the plans of their children to enter imprudent marriages. In this grave matter the parents have the right to guide their children with advice, persuasion, requests, and even moderate rebukes, especially when they are still immature in their judgment. Such acts are quite different from unjust threats, or from importune and unjust vexations, to which a coerced will would consent, albeit in a spirit of complete repugnance.[22]

Sanchez (1550-1610) proposed much the same doctrine. He regarded it as more securely tenable that, unless threats or blows or other means aggravate it, reverential fear is not a factor which overwhelms the will of a normal resolute person. The proof for this he saw in the fact that reverential fear does not appear to connote a sufficient force for coercing the will, so that a normal resolute person would thereby suffer intimidation.[23] Hence, if in a given case reverential fear is present, but from another source (extrinsic to mere reverential fear) some additional fear accrues, then it seems that this complex of fears could be more accurately characterized as a qualified reverential fear. So it seems more properly warranted to consider a mere reverential fear simply as a condition of mind consequent upon the normal relationship of an inferior to his superior.

That relationship, since it is a perfectly normal and expected condition, can not be considered as of itself causing any undue influence on the inferior. It may of course easily open the way for other, but different, types of fear. But these types of fear should be considered extrinsic to mere reverential fear, even though they are concurrent with it and result from a single intention of the one who inspires the fears. Furthermore, the passive subject should follow the dictates of mere reverential fear within the limits of conscience, but he has the strict right to question commands which are given under the accompaniment of conditions and actions that raise fears from sources extrinsic to the simple deferential bond of relationship that obtains.

The superior can rightfully expect the inferior to obey his commands, and he can remind the inferior, whenever it is necessary,

---

[22] *Decisiones,* XXIX (1937), 782-783.

[23] Sanchez, *De Matrimonii Sacramento,* lib. IV, disp. VI, n. 7.

of the reverence and the homage required of him. This is but a natural and reasonable use of the right which entails a reciprocal duty of compliance through the manifestation of a filial reverential fear. But if threats, blows, importunities, or vexations are added, then the mere reverential fear takes on a new form. It is then no longer quite the same, and is best called a *qualified* reverential fear. Hence, *qualified* reverential fear can be defined as a mere reverential fear to which have been added threats, blows, importunities, or other vexations, which can sometimes change that fear into grave fear, whether absolute or relative.[24]

Under the term vexations is to be included the factor of a grave and protracted indignation as causing a qualified reverential fear, even when the threat of other grave evils is not present. Hence a person may prudently be considered as having acted from the fear of grave indignation when he has acted from excessive reverence.[25] In some cases the additional threats, vexations, etc., though not in themselves sufficient to constitute a grave fear, could in conjunction with a mere reverential fear constitute a qualified reverential fear. Sanchez suggested a similar idea when he dwelt upon the consideration of "minor threats."[26]

In conclusion, then, it may be stated that a mere reverential fear is a slight fear, but that a qualified reverential fear as defined above may easily imply the presence of a grave fear. Such seems to be the meaning intended in the *"In iure"* discussions on points of law in fairly recent Rotal decisions, as cited above. Few authors make use of the phrase "qualified reverential fear." In view of the nature of the present treatise, and in the light of recent Rotal usage, it was considered imperative to establish this distinction between mere reverential fear and qualified reverential fear. Hence the question is simply one of a convenient terminology. In practice the authors all come to the same general conclusion; if the inflicted fear is grave as measured in relation to the strength or weakness of the character of the passive subject, then the presence of such a fear precludes a true matrimonial consent.

---

[24] Cf. *Decisiones,* XXVIII (1936), 470.

[25] *Decisiones,* XXVIII (1936), 643-644.

[26] *De Matrimonii Sacramento,* Lib. IV, disp. VI, n. 16.

CHAPTER II

HISTORICAL DEVELOPMENT

In the restricted field of force and fear as affecting marriage cases in the Far East, there was very little information found in the sources available to the writer.[1] There are some Papal ordinances, and also some decrees of the Roman Congregations, which deal more or less specifically with the matter. Local synods have little to the point. Finally, in the sources available, it seems there is a complete lack of Rotal cases until 1911. Apparently there is only one adequate explanation, namely, that the Church went through such continually disturbed conditions in the Far East, that a calm jurisprudence of case law could not be built up. Apparently the sending of appeals to the Rota as a court of higher instance was considered too difficult or perhaps even impossible of realization.

ARTICLE 1. SYNOPSIS OF CHURCH HISTORY IN CHINA

John of Monte Corvino (+ 1328), a Franciscan, opened the Church's activities in China, after being received by the Emperor in 1294.[2] But with the fall of the Mongol dynasty in 1368 into the hands of the Mings, the Church disappeared rapidly with scarcely any trace of it remaining.[3]

---

[1] Various collections of Rotal cases were consulted, but no cases from China or the surrounding countries were found either in Pallottini, *Collectio Omnium Conclusionum, et Resolutionum Quae in causis propositis apud Sacram Congregationem Cardinalium S. Concilii Tridentini interpretum prodierunt ab eius institutione anno MDLXIV ad MDCCCLX, distinctis titulis alphabetico ordine per materias digesta* (18 vols., Romae, 1868-1895), or in the *Acta Sanctae Sedis* (41 vols., Romae, 1865-1908), or in several volumes for the years 1750-1890, and particularly in the volumes for the years 1900-1903 and 1906-1907, of the *Thesaurus Resolutionum Sacrae Congregationis Concilii* (167 vols., Romae, 1718-1908), or in the *Bullarium Pontificium Sacrae Congregationis de Propaganda Fide* (8 vols., ed. S. Bayer, Romae, 1839-1858).

[2] Schmidlin-Braun, *Catholic Mission History* (Techny: Mission Press, S. V. D., 1933), p. 234; Wadding, *Annales Minorum seu Trium Ordinum a S. Francisco Institutorum* (3. ed., 29 vols., Quaracchi, 1931-1948), VI, 77.

[3] Schmidlin-Braun, *Catholic Mission History*, pp. 235-236.

More than two centuries later the Jesuits, led by Matteo Ricci (1552-1610), were able to penetrate China, and finally established a permanent residence in Peking, the imperial city, in 1601.[4] From that time onward the Church was never ousted from China, but neither did it enjoy peace for any length of time. Persecutions, internal dissensions, and political disturbances, frequently in combination, interfered with the Church's freedom of action. Besides the frequent and sporadic local persecutions, there were official persecutions in 1617,[5] in 1707,[6] in 1734, 1736-1737,[7] from 1811 to 1825,[8] and in 1857.[9]

Internal dissensions arose in consequence of the right of patronage as claimed by the Portuguese, as a result of the establishment in 1659 of vicariates apostolic to limit this right, and in view of the controversy over Chinese rites. This controversy started before 1600, and ended only with the Constitution *Ex quo* of Benedict XIV (1740-1758) in 1742. From that time on the missions declined.[10]

In the nineteenth century, political disturbances added to the difficulty, such as the Taiping rebellion beginning in 1853, the Tientsin massacre in 1870, the Boxer rebellion in 1900, and the revolution of 1911.[11] Korea and Indo-China had a similar history. In fact, for long periods they were under Chinese rule, and their history was thereby affected.[12] Mongolia and Manchuria were conquerors of China, but eventually were politically absorbed into China.[13]

---

4 *Ibid.*, p. 332.

5 *Ibid.*, pp. 333-334.

6 *Ibid.*, p. 482.

7 *Ibid.*, p. 494.

8 *Ibid.*, pp. 610-611.

9 *Ibid.*, p. 611.

10 *Ibid.*, pp. 475-483; the Constitution of Benedict XIV, *Ex quo*, of July 11, 1742, is in *Codicis Iuris Canonici Fontes*, cura Emi Petri Card. Gasparri editi (9 vols., Romae [postea Civitate Vaticana]: Typis Polyglottis Vaticanis, 1923-1939; Vols. VII-IX, ed. cura et studio Emi Iustiniani Card. Serédi), n. 329 (hereafter cited *Fontes*). For the oath demanded of missionaries against the proscribed rites, see § 27 of the same Constitution.

11 Schmidlin-Braun, *Catholic Mission History*, pp. 611-613.

12 See p. 18, below.

13 Schmidlin-Braun, *Catholic Mission History*, pp. 235 and 612.

ARTICLE 2. DEVELOPMENT OF LAW

Due to the limitations indicated in the previous article, the sources which indicate any development in the doctrine regarding reverential fear in marriage in the Far East must be sought among the documents emanating from Rome, and in the few official statements of law as enacted in the Far East.

SECTION 1. THE COUNCIL OF TRENT

In connection with the question of force and fear the Council of Trent passed two decrees, the one dealing with the impediment of abduction, and the other with the abuse of temporal lords and magistrates in forcing their subjects into specific marriages.

In the former of these decrees the Council clearly formulated abduction as a strict impediment of ecclesiastical law: " . . . between the abductor and the one abducted there can be no marriage so long as she remains in the power of the abductor."[14] The impediment of abduction was thus distinguished from force and fear.[15]

In the latter of these decrees the Council legislated:

> Since it is something singularly execrable to violate the freedom of matrimony, and equally execrable that injustice should come from those from whom justice is expected, the holy council commands all, of whatever rank, dignity and profession they may be, under penalty of anathema to be incurred *ipso facto,* that they do not in any manner whatever, directly or indirectly, compel their subjects or any others whomsoever in any way that will hinder them from contracting marriage freely.[16]

These two conciliar enactments did not imply a change in the doctrine regarding force and fear; they were simply a restatement of the Church's law in protection of full liberty in the contracting of marriage.[17]

---

[14] Conc. Trident., sess. XXIV, *de ref. matrim.*, c. 6; translation by Schroeder, *Canons and Decrees of the Council of Trent* (St. Louis: Herder, 1941), p. 187.

[15] Wernz, *Ius Matrimoniale,* n. 262.

[16] Conc. Trident., sess. XXIV, *de ref. matrim.*, c. 9; translation by Schroeder, *Canons and Decrees of the Council of Trent,* p. 189.

[17] Juarez, *Vis et Metus,* p. 22.

SECTION 2. THE PERIOD 1600-1800

The relevant pontifical acts of the period 1600-1800 consisted for the most part of directives and cautions for assuring the contracting of marriage in accordance with the existing legislation. Only gradually were more specific instructions given as safeguards for the free and unconstrained contracting of marriage, and still later, instructions on the investigations to be made when marriage causes called for a judicial declaration.

On December 23, 1673, Pope Clement X (1670-1676), in the Constitution *Apostolatus officium,* approved the Synod of Tonking, Indo-China (Synodus Tunchinensis), in which the nineteenth canon decreed that monthly instructions should be given the faithful on the impediments which prohibit or invalidate the marriage contract.[18]

The Holy Office in a reply to the bishop of Scutari in Albania, dated July 9, 1750, stated that Christians who gave their daughters in marriage to pagans were to be seriously reprehended, and punished with heavy penalties.[19] Later the Holy Office referred to this reply in an Instruction to the Vicar Apostolic of Szechuan (Sutchuensis), China, dated January 12, 1769. In the Instruction (paragraph III), missionaries were ordered to deny the dispensation for marriage when the parents sought the dispensation (from disparity of cult) for their children under the age of puberty, in order to give them in marriage to the children of infidels, in line with the custom of pre-puberty marriages. The missionary could give the dispensation only after both spouses had attained the age of puberty, had indicated the freedom of their mutual consent, and had complied with the conditions mentioned in the previous Instruction of November 18, 1745 (quoted in the reply of July 9, 1750, as cited above).[20]

The Congregation for the Propagation of the Faith sent an Instruction, dated April 29, 1784, to the Vicar Apostolic of Sze-

---

[18] *Ius Pontificum de Propaganda Fide* (ed. R. de Martinis, Pars prima, 7 vols. in 8, 1888-1897, Pars secunda, vol. unic., 1909, Romae: Typographia Polyglotta S. C. de Propaganda Fide), Pars I, Vol. I, p. 431, col. 1 (hereafter cited *IP de PF*).

[19] *Fontes,* n. 802.

[20] *Fontes,* n. 822.

chuan, which dealt with several questions, among which was the question of persons incurring the excommunication enacted by the Council of Trent for abducting and transporting to the home of the spouse a girl who had been engaged by her parents to an infidel.[21] The Instruction stated that, if the girl had not attained the use of reason when the parents made the marriage engagement, and did not later upon attaining the use of reason ratify that action of her parents, then the engagement was invalid, and those who had part in the abduction incurred the excommunication; on the contrary, if the girl consented (after puberty) to the engagement, or later ratified it, the engagement was valid, and those who had transported the girl, even against her will, did not come under the excommunication.[22]

Since the decree *Tametsi*[23] had not been promulgated in China, a question was asked relative to what value certain local customs in the civil marriage ceremony in Tonkin, Indo-China, had in determining the presence and extent of marriage consent. The Sacred Congregation for the Propagation of the Faith replied on April 5, 1785, that each case of (clandestine) marriage was to be judged on its own merits, and that the missionary was carefully to establish that in each marriage, contracted or to be contracted, the consent was internal, mutual, expressed by words or other sense-perceptible signs, fully deliberate, free, and immune from grave unjust fear.[24]

SECTION 3. THE NINETEENTH CENTURY

At the beginning of the nineteenth century, during a fairly long interval between official persecutions, an important synod was held at Chungking, in the province of Szechuan, China—in Latin terminology, *Synodus Vicariatus Sutchuensis, habita in districtu civitatis Tcong King Tcheou, d. 2, 5, et 9, Sept. 1803.*[25] In Chapter IX, § III, this Synod dealt with three questions in which freedom

---

[21] Conc. Trident., sess. XXIV, *de ref. matrim.*, c. 6.

[22] *Fontes,* n. 4598, p. 145.

[23] Conc. Trident, sess. XXIV, *de ref. matrim.*, c. 1.

[24] *IP de PF,* Pars II, p. 406; *Fontes,* n. 4601.

[25] *Acta et Decreta Sacrorum Conciliorum Recentiorum, Collectio Lacensis* (7 vols., Friburgi Brisgoviae: Herder, 1870-1892), VI, 592-638 (hereafter cited *Collectio Lacensis*).

of consent was involved. These questions referred to: a) marriage engagements for children under the age of seven; b) marriage engagements for children under the age of puberty; c) marriage engagements made when the parents were still pagans.[26]

a) *Children Under the Age of Seven*

> We forbid parents to make marriage engagements for their children who have not yet completed their seventh year of age. If, to avoid the danger of promising these same children to pagans, or for other similar grave causes, it should sometimes be expedient that such engagements be made, the missionaries shall take care that an express clause be added that they shall not be valid, and that they shall not have any effect, unless the children having attained the years of discretion, shall, with full freedom, have consented.

b) *Children Under the Age of Puberty*

The Synod exhorted parents to refrain from making pre-puberty engagements for their children, stating:

> We strongly exhort the same parents to refrain from contracting such engagements until their children shall have come to the age of puberty, so that they may avoid the many inconveniences and dangers of dissensions which not infrequently occur when there is question of rescinding the contract.[27]

It is clear that marriage engagements made for children who had not attained the age of puberty, or, worse still, who had not attained the age of reason, frequently paved the way for a misuse of the parental authority when the time came for the fulfilling of the contract, let alone the further question which obtained when the parents had been in the wrong when they first made the contract. The repudiation of such contracts was usually very difficult, as the Synod of Szechuan stated in the passage just quoted.

The Synod then gave its legislation on the matter of marriage engagements of children under the age of puberty:

---

[26] *Collectio Lacensis,* VI, 621.
[27] *Collectio Lacensis, loc. cit.*

> If, however (the parents) should wish to contract (the engagement) before this age (of puberty), and the children consent, we command again that it be done with the express clause that either of the affianced parties be free to repudiate the engagement immediately after puberty, if he (or she) does not agree to it. Wherefore, to protect this liberty for all parties, the missionaries shall take care that the said clause shall be put in a document of such nature that it will have legal value before the civil magistrate.
>
> c) *Engagements Made While Parents Were Still Pagans*
>
> With regard to marriage engagements contracted in infidelity, the parents shall never, on account of them, force their children, even though only catechumens, into a marriage when they are unwilling; rather, they should try in all prudence for a dissolution of the engagement; if they cannot obtain it, they shall not give their children in marriage unless the children are willing, their faith not in jeopardy, and besides, a legitimate dispensation shall have been obtained, if the children were already baptized.

Obviously many parents, caught in the dilemma of breaking the engagement under extreme difficulty, or of forcing the unwilling child into the marriage, chose the latter solution. That this practice was not only widespread but also of long standing is indicated by the fact that the Council of Shanghai had to take up the question again in 1924, severely censuring marriage engagements for children who were in infancy or had not yet attained puberty.[28]

The Holy Office on April 9, 1851, answered a question on a case involving forced marriage consent. A Catholic boy, aged 18, did not care for the girl chosen by his mother to be his wife. The mother was a recent convert. After unsuccessfully urging her son, the mother threatened in anger to abandon (in the original French, *abandonnerait*) her son, to return to live with her pagan parents, and to give up her (Catholic) religion. The boy there-

[28] *Primum Concilium Sinense, Anno 1924 . . . Celebratum: Acta—Decreta et Normae—Vota etc.* (Zi-ka-wei: Typographia Missionis Catholicae [T'ou-se-we], 1929), n. 381 (hereafter cited *Council of Shanghai*).

upon consented. The Holy Office replied that in such a case grave fear was not present.[29]

The boy refused to have anything to do with his wife after the marriage, and showed an aversion for her. Yet this was not sufficient to establish the fact that grave fear had existed before the marriage. Hence there is the indicated caution that in cases of this type the mere threat of abandoning the child cannot be considered as causing grave fear, in spite of the fact that what was threatened was of serious consequence in China.[30] Perhaps, in the case, it was not sufficiently proved that the mother could and would have carried out her threat.

The Holy Office, on September 12, 1855, answered a question about masters giving their female servants to various men successively. The question came from Korea, and stated in substance that, among infidels, slaves did not contract marriage properly so-called, for the master who had a marriageable maid-servant would simply call upon a willing man to live as husband with her, though the woman was never asked for her consent. The man was not held by any bond. He could depart at his pleasure. In consequence the woman was successively joined to several men in the same manner. The proponent of the question had declared that these "lecherous unions" did not have the nature of marriage. The reply of the Holy Office approved this decision, with the proviso that in these marriages no reciprocal matrimonal consent had been given before baptism.[31]

The Holy Office issued an Instruction in 1883 to the Bishops of the Oriental Rites,[32] and the Congregation for the Propagation of the Faith issued a very similar and almost identical Instruction in the same year.[33] In these Instructions numbers 36 to 40 treated of what then was called the impediment of force and fear. A detailed analysis was given regarding the various sources of proof for and against the fact of force and fear as being involved in a

---

29 *Collectanea Constitutionum, Decretorum, Indultorum ac Instructionum Sanctae Sedis ad usum Operariorum Apostolicorum Societatis Missionum ad Exteros* (Parisiis, 1880), p. 435, col. 1 (n. 964).

30 See p. 19, below.

31 *Fontes,* n. 934.

32 *Fontes,* n. 1076.

33 *Fontes,* n. 4901.

given marriage. Such sources of proof were rooted in various factors: the power and the character of the one who inflicted the force and fear, the character of the one who suffered the force and fear, the circumstances before, during, and after the marriage ceremony, the character and the credibility of the witnesses, etc. No discussion of principles was offered, nor was any relative evaluation of the types of proof indicated. The Instructions looked solely to the question of judicial procedure.

It is interesting to note that when at a later time the Instruction was reissued on February 18, 1929, to China, shortly after the celebration of the Council of Shanghai, a short significant phrase was added to a sentence in the first paragraph.[34] The sentence, with the addition in italics, is as follows: "The party who has lived in the marriage for a long time is to be rejected, provided he did not lack the liberty and opportunity of suing, *granted that he was conscious of the nullity of the marriage.*" This was the only significant change in the new Instruction, and hence furnished no further development in the doctrine on force and fear.

SECTION 4. ROTA CASES TO 1918

No attempt has been made to find any development in the authors on the question of reverential fear. Even the terminology showed little development, the doctrine itself remaining settled. From the time of Gregory IX "no positive change occurred in the legislation, and whole question resolved itself into one of the *praxis Ecclesiae*."[35] Sanchez (d. 1610) was the classical author on the doctrine regarding matrimony, and later authors followed him for the most part.[36]

In the *Acta Apostolicae Sedis* and in the published series *Sacrae Romanae Rotae Decisiones seu Sententiae* there were found only four Rota cases relative to marriage that dealt with force and fear in the Chinese-culture group of nations in the period 1909-1918. The judicial acts of one of these cases do not even use the term "reverential fear," though that type of fear was in-

[34] *Council of Shanghai*, p. 298, n. 34.
[35] Sangmeister, *Force and Fear*, p. 70.
[36] Juarez, *Vis et Metus*, p. 23.

volved.[37] In another, reverential fear was acknowledged as grave in view of the attendant circumstances.[38] In a third, reverential fear was accounted as a grave fear on condition that some additional factor intervened, e. g., vexations, threats, quarrels, importunate and protracted pleadings and urgings.[39] In only one case was there an actual use of the term *qualified,* and it was employed in the sense that under attending modifying factors the reverential fear could (as it actually did in the case) connote the presence of a grave fear.[40]

SECTION 5. INFLUENCE OF CHINESE LAW CONCEPTS

A short discussion on Chinese law, and on the relationship between parent and child as it exists in China, may be added here. The writer does not propose to examine the field of social custom. Rather, this section will simply consider a few points on the concepts underlying Chinese law, in order to illustrate the relationship between parent and child.

According to the traditional concept in China, law is not differentiated from ethics; in fact, law merely puts ethics into practice. The law is merely a criterion of repression. If in other countries ethical rules intervene only in order to complete the force of juridical precepts, in China the juridical precept intervenes only to give full force to the ethical rules.[41] The ancient ethical theories kept their value from former times up to the present, when the present civil code was promulgated by sections, in the 1920's.

In such a conception there was place only for penal law. Two main reasons were given. The first was that, as a result of successful military expeditions into neighboring countries, the prestige, social hierarchy and rule of the Chinese had to be enforced by means of penal law.[42] Secondly, the law had to be penal in

---

[37] *Acta Apostolicae Sedis, Commentarium Officiale* (Romae, 1909—), V, (1913), 254-255 (hereafter cited *AAS*)—*Decisiones,* V (1913), 54-55.

[38] *AAS,* III (1911), 663; *Decisiones,* III (1911), 334.

[39] *AAS,* IX (1917), 505; *Decisiones,* IX (1917), 25.

[40] *AAS,* V (1913), 556; *Decisiones,* V (1913), 464.

[41] Escarra, *Le Droit Chinois* (Pekin: Editions Henri Vetch, 1936), p. 70.

[42] *Op. cit.,* p. 71.

character in order to intimidate those who gave obedience to the natural and the ethical order for no other motive than that of punishment. Indeed, extreme penalties were enacted, but they were not always religiously applied.[43]

Even today, responsibility is not looked upon as necessarily deriving from the fact that a legal obligation has been violated. In China the idea is that the basis of an infringement (with the consequence of responsibility) consists in an attack upon the natural (i. e., the moral) order. For this reason the heightened concept of the natural order along with a profound consciousness regarding the social hierarchy takes the place of thè idea of law.[44]

In the West, the jurisconsults have built, in the course of ages, a work both of analysis and of synthesis, a body of legal doctrine which constantly tends to clarify and to perfect the technical elements of the positive juridical system. The same does not obtain in the Far East. China has given the law a secondary place, and in this, as in other instances, she has influenced also the neighboring countries: Korea, Japan, Indo-China, Siam, and Burma. Throughout her juridical institutions China has recognized only the natural order, and exalted only the "reign of morality." The designated sanctions, being essentially only penal, but at the same time extremely severe, played above all a role of intimidation. Hence the state and its delegate, the judge, saw their influence weakened in the face of the great power of the head of the clan, the *father of the family,* the administrator in general. This great power evinced its force in the respective fields by settling conflicts according to equity, usage, and local custom.[45]

From the foregoing analysis it appears that, according to the Chinese concept, law is penal in its nature, and subsidiary to rather than co-ordinate with the moral and the natural order. The indicated penalties are indeed severe, but they are considered more as a threat in reserve, according to the principle: "Punish to avoid punishing."[46]

---

[43] *Op. cit.*, p. 73.

[44] *Op. cit.*, p. 77.

[45] *Op. cit.*, p. 4.

[46] *Op. cit.*, p. 18—citing the classics *Shu ching,* L. XXI, and *Chün Ch'eng,* III, § 9, and referring to the translation in "Legge, *Chinese Classics,* Vol. III, part 2, pp. 541-542."

Secondly, there follows the important conclusion that the head of the clan, and the father of the family, will by reason of his great power exercise a strong influence on the child when making the choice of a partner in marriage for the child. This is exemplified in the following statement: "It is to be remarked first of all that it is the parents who choose the wives for their sons, and the husbands for their daughters." This statement was made by the judge of the ecclesiastical court in Tonkin.[47]

There is nothing extraordinary in the practice whereby the parents make the choice for the child, since the child, in consequence of its thorough training in filial piety, will usually accept the arrangement without question. Even if the child dislikes the other party, it will accept the decision of the parents in reverential deference to their wish, as was outlined at the beginning of this treatise. The particular danger that can arise becomes manifest when the child is strongly opposed to the arrangement, and the parents use unjustified pressure on the filial piety of the child. If the parents, furthermore, threaten to disown the child, it must be noted that such a threat often amounts to a threat of complete ostracism from the family, and automatically also from the clan. Such ostracism in China normally implies a terrible lot for its victim.[48]

In making such a threat the parent is acting on a basis similar to that which underlies the *legal* attitude of intimidation: there is present the need of invoking severe penalties for the disrupting of the natural order, in this case the dire disruption of the settled relationship between child and parent. Evidently a qualified reverential fear would thus be present, and it could easily be grave in character.

The modern Chinese Civil Code officially protects the freedom of the parties in betrothal and marriage. By Article 972: "An agreement to marry shall be made by the male and the female parties of their own accord." By Article 997: "A person who has been induced by fraud or by duress to conclude a marriage

---

[47] *AAS,* III (1911), 663; *Decisiones,* III (1911), 334.
[48] *AAS,* III (1911), 665; *Decisiones,* III (1911), 336.

may apply to the Court for its annulment within six months after the discovery of the fraud or after the cessation of the duress."[49] But the matrimonial legislation of the Chinese Civil Code is something new in China. The immense majority of the people, since they do not live in the great cities that have foreign contacts, ignore these regulations, and in all probability will continue to ignore them for the future.[50]

Catholic parents will continue to be influenced by this traditional concept of the power of the father to dictate matrimonial arrangements, and to use the threat of disowning or of ostracizing a child which does not comply with their wish. The exercise of such power in connection with such threats can, it seems clear, often have the same or even greater influence than blows, or any other types of threats and importunities, in giving rise to a qualified reverential fear, and indeed one which not infrequently connotes the presence of a great and overpowering fear.

---

[49] *The Civil Code of the Republic of China,* translated by Ching-lin Hsia, James L. E. Chow, Liu Chieh, Yukon Chang (Shanghai: Kelly and Walsh, 1931), pp. 251 and 257.

[50] Escarra, *Le Droit Chinois,* pp. 184-185.

Part Two—Canonical Commentary

CHAPTER I

CANON 1087: CONDITIONS FOR INVALIDITY

The present chapter will examine the various conditions for invalidity of a marriage from force and fear, as indicated in canon 1087:

> § 1. *Invalidum quoque est matrimonium initum ob vim vel metum gravem ab extrinseco et iniuste incussum, a quo ut quis se liberet, eligere cogatur matrimonium.*
> § 2. *Nullus alius metus, etiamsi det causam contractui, matrimonii nullitatem secumfert.*

Since the principles of force and fear have already been discussed in Part One of this dissertation, the present chapter will deal with the applications of these principles.

Article 1. Force

Physical (or absolute) extrinsic force excludes the matrimonial consent given solely under its influence, and consequently makes the attempted marriage invalid.[1] An act placed under such conditions is plainly not an *actus humanus,* but an act entirely contradicting the internal will of the person affected, and hence has no value as consent,[2] since it has neither moral nor juridical value,[3] or, as Reiffenstuel phrased it, "inasmuch as it is done by force, the interior will does nothing."[4] Even if the party so forced should

---

[1] Can. 103, § 1; cf. Coronata, *De Matrimonio,* n. 466.

[2] Cappello, *De Matrimonio,* n. 606; *AAS,* III (1911) 662; *Decisiones,* III (1911), 333.

[3] Gasparri, *Tractatus Canonicus de Matrimonio* (ed. nova ad mentem Codicis I. C., 2 vols., Romae: Typis Polyglottis Vaticanis, 1932), Vol. II, n. 832 (hereafter cited *De Matrimonio*). Gasparri here quoted the Decretals: "Since (the party so acting) is shown to be acted upon rather than acting." —C. 5, X, *de his, quae vi metusve causa fiunt,* I, 40. Cf. also *Decisiones,* XXII (1930), 654.

[4] *Ius Canonicum Universum* (5 vols. in 4, Monachii, 1702-1710), Lib. I, tit. 40, n. 3. He also quoted the same passage from the Decretals as Gasparri (see previous footnote).

happen to give internal consent at the moment the external act of consent was made, it would still be of no value, since the external act, produced by force, would not be a true sign of free internal consent.[5]

Coronata mentions that ordinarily there could hardly be a case in which the consent became vitiated through the use of physical force, but he notes a possible exception in a case from Korea.[6] This case was decided by the Rota in 1913.[7] In the *Quod ad ius pertinet* discussion it was stated: "[Besides the principles given we might discuss] whether in this case violence, taken in the stricter sense, was present, or only in the wider sense, as grave fear; and therefore whether the marriage is null only from the impediment of force or fear, or rather because the assent was entirely lacking in the marriage."[8]

The facts of the case show that on the morning of the marriage the girl ran away and hid herself twice, before she was finally pushed to the altar. Upon sharp questioning by the priest concerning her consent, she ran away from the altar. Her father caught her and beat her with a stick. She was led back to the altar, where her father and others kept urging, "Answer, 'I do'." In this confusion she did not know what she said, amid her tears and sobs, but only after the Mass heard that she had contracted marriage.[9]

The court also stated that if any case presented to it was easy to solve, this certainly was, on account of so many and such varied acts of violence inflicted on the girl; furthermore, the constancy of the girl against the force used before, during, and after the marriage left no doubt that she in no wise gave consent; even if consent had been there, the marriage would be null on account of the diriment impediment [of fear].[10] The term "diri-

[5] Cf. Coronata, *De Matrimonio,* n. 466, and Gasparri, *De Matrimonio,* n. 832.

[6] *De Matrimonio,* n. 466, with footnote, n. 5.

[7] *AAS,* V (1913), 253-261; *Decisiones,* V (1913), 53-61.

[8] *AAS, ibid.,* p. 255; *Decisiones, ibid.,* p. 55.

[9] *AAS, ibid.,* pp. 256-257; *Decisiones, ibid.,* pp. 55-57—summarized testimony of the girl only, but confirmed in detail by other witnesses.

[10] *AAS, ibid.,* p. 259; *Decisiones; ibid.,* p. 59.

ment impediment" was here used in the wider sense, as including impediments improperly so called. This usage persists.[11]

In connection with this case, it is to be pointed out that canon 1087 does not consider absolute force, which takes away the *voluntarium* by exerting physical force which cannot be successfully resisted by the unwilling party. The force referred to in canon 1087 is moral (or conditional) force, which is the direct cause of fear.[12]

There is no need for canon 1087 to include absolute force or the type of fear which absolutely impedes deliberation, choice and consent, since canon 1081, § 1, already states: "Marriage is contracted by the legitimately manifested *consent* of the parties . . . ." Hence canon 1087 deals with fear that does not take away liberty, but lessens it. Anyone who consents through fear, to avoid some evil, gives an incomplete consent, and consents with repugnance and quasi-unwillingness.[13]

In the Rota case just discussed, then, it is obvious that invalidity would have to be declared, either from lack of consent (by canon 1081), or from vitiated consent (by canon 1087).[14] The court decided that consent was entirely lacking: "There can be no doubt that she in no wise gave consent to the marriage; even if the consent had been there, the marriage would have been null, on account of the diriment impediment [of fear]."[15]

In another case, from Tonkin (Indo-China), the Rota suggested that consent was entirely lacking, but decided for nullity on the head of force and fear vitiating the consent that might have been present.[16]

In a comparatively recent case, from China proper, the element of physical force was so strong that there was doubt about the giving of any consent at all.[17] Payen did not discuss the case,

---

[11] Cf. *Decisiones,* XXVI (1934), 761; XXIX (1937), 40; Coronata, *De Matrimonio,* n. 288; Gasparri, *De Matrimonio,* n. 205.

[12] Payen, *De Matrimonio in Missionibus ac potissimum in Sinis* (2. ed., 3 vols., Zi-ka-wei: In Typographia T'ou-se-we, 1935-1936), II, n. 1678 (hereafter cited *De Matrimonio*).

[13] Payen, *De Matrimonio,* II, n. 1679.

[14] Payen, *De Matrimonio,* II, n. 1701.

[15] *AAS,* V (1913), 259; *Decisiones,* V (1913), 59.

[16] *AAS,* III (1911), 662 and 666; *Decisiones,* III (1911), 333 and 337.

[17] *Decisiones,* XXII (1930), 652-662.

since his work on Matrimony was published in 1935, three years before the volume of Rota decisions of 1930 was published in 1938. In this case the Rota commented on the unusual harshness shown. A summary of its comment on this point is as follows: These events were such an abnormal thing among the Chinese people that the catechist, on account of the improper manner in which the girl was brought into the chapel, refused to assist the priest (as witness), and testified: "All the indignant onlookers cursed because of the improper manner of dealing with the girl." Another witness declared: "All who were present at the celebration of this marriage were unanimous in expressing their anger: 'It is not right for the Sisters to force the plaintiff in this manner to celebrate the marriage'."[18]

That physical force was used before, during, and after the ceremony, is clear from the testimony, as a few selections from it will show. The girl was from an orphanage under the care of the Sisters. A marriage had been arranged for her by the priest in charge. She objected strongly to the arrangement. On the day of the marriage she was forcibly led to the doors of the chapel. There, seized by the arms and pushed by blows from behind, she was forced to the altar amid her weeping and sobbing. During the actual celebration of the marriage, when the girl denied consent, the Sisters forced her by blows to bow her head, and they pulled her ears. When the priest urged her to express consent, she, in anger, after further blows, used a phrase that had no meaning of consent. After refusing to join her right hand with that of the man, she threw the wedding ring to the ground twice, after it had been put on her finger.[19]

The Rota approved the decision of the lower court, which had stated that the plaintiff had given consent only as impelled by force, but indeed a false consent, which indicated and proved the nullity of the marriage for the lack of consent. The decision of the Rota supported this sentence for the nullity of the marriage, and the sentence of the Rota was made *exsecutiva*.[20] The Rota stated that the case furnished sufficient arguments for the nullity of the marriage on the score of force and fear (in line with the

---

[18] *Ibid.*, p. 660.
[19] *Ibid.*, pp. 653; 656-659.
[20] *Ibid.*, pp. 661-662.

ruling of canon 1087). But it added that the assertion of the girl that she had not given consent was also sufficiently proved, so that the marriage could also have been declared invalid for lack of consent (in line with the ruling of canon 1081, § 1).[21]

The writer has selected the two cases examined above in order to show that in rare cases physical force was applied to such an extent that in all likelihood no consent at all was given by the injured party. The kind of force used in the cases here mentioned comes very close to satisfying the definition and description given by St. Thomas, who stated that absolute force affects external acts, and cannot be repelled, either because the use of reason is taken away or because the victim cannot resist the force.[22] St. Bonaventure's description is more vivid: "Physical force is placed when the unwilling party is seized, led, dragged, or bound, while he protests and objects; this is a coercion (*coactio*) in which there is no consent, and there is absolutely no marriage."[23]

Article 2. Fear or Moral Force

Section 1. General Notions on Fear

Marriage is also invalid if contracted under the influence of force or grave fear which an outside agency unjustly exercised over a person so that he was forced to choose marriage as a means to free himself from the force or fear. No other fear entails the nullity of marriage though it caused the contract to be made. (Canon 1087, §§ 1-2).[24]

---

[21] *Ibid.*, p. 661. For other examples of physical force which, though they did not suffice to evince an entire lack of consent, gave proof of force and fear according to the ruling of canon 1087, see *AAS*, IX (1917), 505; *Decisiones*, IX (1917), 25-26; *Decisiones*, XVIII (1926), 156; *Decisiones*, XIII (1921), 252. This last case, however, contained the observation (p. 252): "There is question not only of reverential fear as inflicted by the mother of the daughter, but also of common fear, and even of force (*vi*) properly so-called, as having been inflicted."

[22] In Lib. IV Sent., d. 22, q. 1, a. 1—cited by the Rota in another case: *AAS*, III (1911), 662; *Decisiones*, III (1911), 333.

[23] In Lib. IV Sent., d. 29, a. 1, q. 1—*Opera Omnia* (10 vols. in 11, Quaracchi, 1882-1902), Vol. IV, p. 699.

[24] Translation from Woywod-Smith, *A Practical Commentary on the Code of Canon Law* (2. ed., 10th printing, 2 vols., New York: Joseph Wagner, 1946), I, 654-655 (hereafter cited *Commentary*).

Hence for fear to invalidate marriage it must: 1) be grave; 2) derive from an extrinsic and free cause; 3) be unjustly inflicted, and 4) be such that one has no escape from it except by choosing marriage. These points will be dealt with in turn. Reverential fear, which may involve any or all of these points, but which in addition raises special problems of its own, will be considered in a separate chapter.

SECTION 2. GRAVE FEAR

Grave fear, in the classical definition, is that which befalls a resolute person—"*qui cadit in virum constantem.*"[25] In general, the threatening evil must be grave for the particular person who fears it, and he must be convinced that this evil really threatens him.[26] Fear results from a threatening evil,[27] and if this evil is to cause a grave fear it must itself be grave and certainly threatening.[28]

A. *Gravity of the Evil*

Certain evils are considered as grave in themselves. Such evils are death, mutilation, slavery, exile, loss of goods, or forfeiture of the reputation to which one has a right.[29] But the reaction of persons to threatening evils is different according to the person's character, abilities, upbringing, etc. The distinction between absolutely grave and relatively grave fear must be kept in mind. An evil that is not grave in itself may bring about a strong fear in the person affected, and this type of fear is called relatively grave. Since it is grave for the person affected, it would be sufficient to satisfy the requisite of grave fear which invalidates marriage. The phrase, "*cadens in virum constantem,*" must be understood in this sense. A Rota case, originating in Tonkin, Indo-China,[30] made this comment on the phrase: "This phrase, according to

---

[25] D. (4, 2) 1, 6; Cc. 15, 28, X, *de sponsalibus et matrimoniis,* IV, 1.

[26] Gasparri, *De Matrimonio,* n. 846; Sangmeister, *Force and Fear,* p. 100; Coronata, *De Matrimonio,* n. 470.

[27] Cf. D. (4, 2) 2.

[28] Reiffenstuel, Lib. I, tit. 40, n. 19.

[29] Coronata, *De Matrimonio,* n. 470.

[30] *Decisiones,* XVI (1924), 164.

Sanchez [1550-1610],[31] is to be properly understood, namely, 'when one speaks of fear befalling a resolute man, one understands that strength of character which attaches to an individual in accord with his condition and state in life."[32] In other words, the gravity is to be measured and appraised not absolutely, but relatively to the person influenced. Outlook, age, sex, and other circumstantial factors call for their due consideration. The fear is grave, if with reference to the nature of the evil in relation to the person affected it exists for that person as a constraining force which within reason he feels unable to counteract.[33] The fear must befall a person who is resolute in this relative sense.[34]

B. *Certainty of the Threat*

The affected party must be convinced, at least through a moral certainty induced in the light of the normally expected human propensities, that the evil will be incurred. If there is to be established a full certainty of the threat, three conditions must be fulfilled: first, the threatening agent must be thought of as able to carry out the threat; secondly, he must be regarded as a person who regularly carries out his threat, even an unusual one, in view of his dominance of resolve; thirdly, the victim must be unable to sense anything but marriage as a means for eluding the threatened evil.[35]

The fear is grave whether the evil threatens the party himself or those with whom he is closely bound by relationship, friendship, etc., provided that the fear is at least relatively grave, as explained above.[36]

---

[31] Cf. *De Matrimonii Sacramento,* Lib. IV, disp. III, n. 4.

[32] *"Dum dicitur metus cadens in virum constantem, intelligitur * nonnisi virium robur * pro cuiusque conditione."* This wording is from the Rota case. However, in the three Sanchez editions available to the writer (Genevae, 1602; Antverpiae, 1626; Venetiis, 1607), the wording is *nomine viri, animi robur,* instead of the words set off with the asterisks.

[33] *Decisiones,* XVI (1924), 139.

[34] Payen, *De Matrimonio,* II, n. 1682, (3).

[35] Reiffenstuel, Lib. I, tit. 40, n. 19.

[36] Cf. Coronata, *De Matrimonio,* n. 470; Gasparri, *De Matrimonio,* n. 847; Juarez, *Vis et Metus,* p. 29.

SECTION 3. EXTRINSIC AND FREE CAUSE

For the nullity of the marriage it is postulated that the fear be caused by an extrinsic and free agent. An intrinsic cause is a necessary cause, natural or supernatural; it prescinds from the notion of a free human agent's intervention.[37] A supernatural cause is evinced through the fear of hell or a troubled conscience which harkens to past sins or injustices. Natural causes are exemplified in a danger to health, in exposure to extreme poverty, in the risk of infamy, in the hazard of imprisonment, etc.[38]

The extrinsic cause postulated in canon 1087, § 1, is a free cause. Since only a free cause can act unjustly, it is from man that the threat of the evil must originate.[39] The free human agent may be the other party of the proposed marriage, or the parents, the relatives, or any one at all. The Church's established rule regarding the nullity of a marriage which is contracted by anyone who is victimized with grave fear reflects not only the Church's condemnation of the unjust infliction of fear, but also the Church's desire fully to certify the freedom of people in the contracting of marriage.[40]

SECTION 4. FEAR UNJUSTLY INFLICTED

In order to affect the validity of a marriage, the fear must be unjustly inflicted. In this respect the authors do not agree in their analysis of exactly what constitutes the unjust infliction of fear. They differ widely in their comprehension of the types of unjust infliction, as will be seen shortly in a comparison of the doctrines of Payen (+ 1941) and Coronata.

In order to discuss properly the notion of the unjust infliction of fear one must advert in particular to two principles. Real injury is not inflicted by one who in the enjoyment of a right exercises it lawfully. Secondly, with reference to the question of validity or invalidity for a marriage, it is justice alone, and not any other virtue, that is involved in the inflicting of the fear.[41]

---

[37] Coronata, *De Matrimonio*, n. 469.

[38] Coronata, *loc. cit.;* Payen, *De Matrimonio*, II, n. 1684.

[39] Coronata, *loc. cit.*; Payen, *loc. cit.*

[40] Payen, *loc. cit.;* Reiffenstuel, Lib. IV, tit. 1, n. 327; Capello, *De Matrimonio*, n. 607.

[41] Cf. Sangmeister, *Force and Fear*, p. 107.

The authors admit the difficulty of determining the exact notion of the unjust infliction of fear. They approach the problem by distinguishing between fear unjustly inflicted in substance and fear unjustly inflicted in manner.[42]

Fear is unjustly inflicted in substance if an evil is inflicted on or threatened for a person who does not deserve it, and thus becomes deprived of his rights through a violation of the claims of justice, or at least of strict justice.[43] Coronata makes a much different approach. He claims that fear is just in substance if the law recognizes the legal right to use coercion on someone in certain cases, such as the "marriage or jail" sentences sometimes given by judges in the United States.[44] In the present section, which deals with the unjustly inflicted fear, the writer follows Payen's opinion for the most part, and adopts his definitions.

Fear is unjustly inflicted in manner if the evil is inflicted or threatened in an improper and undue fashion, as would happen if a sentence were rendered by a judge who does not have competency in the case, or if a sentence abstracted from the observance of the requisite legal formalities, from the execution of the essential rules of procedure, or from the needed reliance upon sufficient proofs.[45] Under this heading (unjustly in manner) some authors include the infliction of exorbitant penalties,[46] but it rather seems that such an act redounds to an unjust infliction in substance, since the inflicting agent has no right at all, even fundamentally, to inflict such excessive penalties. Payen adverted to the actual existence of this opinion, though he himself did not adhere to it:

---

42 Payen, *De Matrimonio,* II, n. 1685; Sangmeister, *Force and Fear,* p. 108; Coronata, *De Matrimonio,* n. 472. Cappello (*De Matrimonio,* n. 607) claims that this distinction is no longer of any value, since the Code now uses the adverb *iniuste* in canon 1087. This point will be discussed shortly. Cf. also *Decisiones,* XIV (1922), 79.

43 Payen, *De Matrimonio,* II, n. 1685.

44 *De Matrimonio,* n. 472.

45 Payen, *De Matrimonio,* II, n. 1685; Sangmeister, *Force and Fear,* pp. 108-109.

46 Payen, *De Matrimonio,* II, n. 1685; Wernz-Vidal, *Ius Canonicum* (7 vols. in 8, Romae: Universitas Gregoriana, 1923-1938; Vol. II, *De Personis,* 3. ed., recognovit P. Aguirre, 1943; Vol. V, *Ius Matrimoniale,* 3. ed., recognovit P. Aguirre, 1946), V, *Ius Matrimoniale,* n. 501, note 24 (hereafter cited *Ius Matrimoniale*).

"The controversy (which is involved once this distinction is accepted between unjust infliction in substance or in manner) is of no moment if one considers every grave fear exercised by a judge when he seeks to bring about a marriage as being unjustly inflicted *in substance.*"[47]

If the distinction between substance and manner in the just or unjust infliction of fear is accepted, four possible combinations arise. These will now be considered in turn.[48]

A) *Fear, Just in Substance and Manner*

Obviously the infliction of this type of fear would not affect the validity of the marriage, for the one who thus inflicts the fear is within his rights; the rights of the affected party have not been attacked. Such a case would be exemplified if a father, in threatening suit for damages, gave his daughter's seducer the choice either of marrying her or of paying reasonable damages (the amount would be equivalent to a reasonable dowry).[49]

B) *Fear, Unjust in Substance and Manner*

In this case the inflicted fear obviously *does* affect the validity of the marriage, because it is clearly *iniuste incussum.* A man unjustly accused of seduction, and forced at pistol-point to go through a marriage ceremony, would have contracted an invalid marriage.

C) *Fear, Unjust in Substance But Just in Manner*

In this case the inflicted fear would cause invalidity because the one inflicting the fear would have no grounds for his action, even though he used the proper legal channels. If a judge forced the choice either of marriage or of the payment of heavy damages upon a man juridically proved guilty of seduction but in fact

---

[47] Payen, *De Matrimonio,* II, n. 1685. Sangmeister (*Force and Fear,* p. 126) refers to Payen on this point, and with him rejects the opinion which regards the judge's act of compelling the giving of a matrimonial consent as involving in substance, and not only in manner, the unjust infliction of fear.

[48] Cf. Sangmeister, *Force and Fear,* p. 117.

[49] Cappello, *De Matrimonio,* n. 607; Sangmeister, *Force and Fear,* pp. 110-111.

innocent, he would be inflicting fear justly in manner but not in substance.

D) *Fear, Just in Substance But Unjust in Manner*

This category is subject to dispute among the authors, but the opinion apparently gaining ground is that which holds that fear, even if gravely unjust in manner only, is sufficient to invalidate a marriage, precisely because the Code in canon 1087 uses the adverbial form *iniuste.* The Code does not distinguish between substance and manner in the injustice which motivates the infliction of the fear but merely refers to fear *unjustly* inflicted. Now, whether the fear is unjust in its infliction either in substance or in manner, it is *unjustly* inflicted, and satisfies the terminology of the Code.[50]

The opposite opinion, that fear unjust only in manner would not invalidate marriage was held by some authors.[51]

The writer follows the opinion which claims that the phrase

---

[50] Cappello, *De Matrimonio,* n. 607; Coronata, *De Matrimonio,* n. 472; Chelodi-Ciprotti, *Ius Canonicum de Matrimonio et de Iudiciis Matrimonialibus* (5. ed., Vicenza: Società Anonima Tipografica, 1947), n. 119 (hereafter cited *De Matrimonio*); Juarez, *Vis et Metus,* p. 33; Payen, *De Matrimonio,* II, n. 1685 (2); Vermeersch-Creusen, *Epitome Iuris Canonici* (5. ed., 3 vols., Mechliniae-Romae, H. Dessain, 1933-1936), II, n. 376 (hereafter cited *Epitome*); Roberti, *De Processibus* (2. ed., third printing, Vol. I, Romae: Libraria Pontificii Instituti Utriusque Iuris, 1941), I, n. 259; Gasparri, *De Matrimonio,* n. 855; *Decisiones,* XXVI (1934), 3, 782.

[51] Genicot-Salsmans, *Institutiones Theologiae Moralis* (11. ed., 2 vols., Bruxellis; Alb. Dewit, 1927), II, n. 463 (II), 3° (hereafter cited *Institutiones*). De Smet formerly held this opinion in his *Tractatus Theologico-Canonicus de Sponsalibus et Matrimonio* (Romae, 1909), pp. 325-326, but after the promulgation of the Code he changed to the more commonly held opinion that fear unjustly inflicted in manner only *does* invalidate marriage, since canon 1087 reads *"metus iniuste incussus"* rather than *"metus iniustus."* Cf. his work *Tractatus Theologico-Canonicus de Sponsalibus et Matrimonio* (4. ed., Brugis: Beyaert, 1927), n. 538 (p. 472), note 5 (hereafter cited *De Sponsalibus et Matrimonio*—for the fourth edition, unless other indication be given). Similarly, Vermeersch-Creusen in the *second* edition of their *Epitome,* II (Mechliniae-Romae, 1925), n. 376, changed to the more commonly held opinion, since "the Code does not speak of unjust fear, but of that which is unjustly inflicted."

"*iniuste incussum*" refers to fear unjustly inflicted, whether in substance or in manner, or in both.

The general principle governing the four categories of fear just discussed should then be: For a marriage to be valid, the fear must be just in substance and in manner. If it is unjust on either count,[52] or on both counts, the marriage is invalid.[53]

One more controverted point may be considered. In some civil jurisdictions, if a man has been proved guilty of having seduced a woman into fornication, the judge is authorized by law to give the man the alternative either of marrying the woman or of going to prison. If the man was actually guilty of rape (*stuprum violentum*), Gasparri (1852-1934) maintained that the fear inflicted through this alternative was just, so that the marriage which was entered into as a result of it was to be regarded as valid. He noted that cognizance of the crime could be taken in either the ecclesiastical or the civil forum, but pointed out that the canonical penalties are relatively less severe.[54]

The same conclusion may be drawn from a Rota case: *"Ei autem cui ex sua culpa a legitimo iudice vel superiore seu ad iuris normam matrimonium imponitur, nulla profecto infertur iniuria: ipse enim revera sibi metum intulit."*[55] This opinion was also held by the Rota with reference to a case in which there was seduction along with the promise of marriage.[56]

Reiffenstuel (1642-1703) mentioned the canonical penalties of the external forum for seduction or rape as being *ducere aut dotare,* and to furnish support for the children begotten through the act of fornication.[57]

The other opinion holds that in the case in question the fear is unjustly inflicted in manner. Obviously the civil penalty ex-

---

52 *Decisiones,* XXVI (1934), 782.

53 Coronata, *De Matrimonio,* n. 472: "*A fortiori autem dicendus erit metus iniustus qui talis fuerit etiam in substantia.*"

54 *De Matrimonio,* n. 853. In the footnote here (note 1), Gasparri cited: "D'Annibale, p. III, § 445, not. 19."

55 *Decisiones,* XXIX (1937), 40.

56 *Decisiones,* XXIX (1937), 71: *Metus iustus reputatur qui a iudice etiam laico incutitur ei qui virginem spe matrimonii defloravit, carceris detrusione comminata nisi defloratam in uxorem ducat.*

57 Lib. IV, tit. 1, nn. 70-72; Lib. V, tit. 16, n. 51.

ceeds the pre-Code penalty in severity. Woywod-Smith gives two cogent reasons for holding this latter opinion. "First, such a law giving the judge the right to demand that alternative is not conducive to the public welfare but rather injurious, for happy marriages are not, as a rule, contracted in that fashion.[58] Furthermore, often an outright injustice is done to the man, since in many cases the woman is equally guilty, according to the old axiom, *scienti et volenti non fit iniuria.*"[59]

The writer agrees with the latter opinion, which is also held by Cappello, who says that the judge is limited to demanding either marriage or dowry (hence, damages).[60] Payen did not treat the case specifically,[61] but referred to, without approving, the rather sweeping conclusion of Vermeersch (1858-1936):[62] *"Immo, cum nunc nulla actio detur ad exigendum ipsum matrimonium,[63] iniustus dicendus est omnis metus ad matrimonium obtinendum incussus."*

SECTION 5. FEAR CAUSING MARRIAGE

Before the fear will invalidate the marriage, it must exist as the cause of the marriage. The fear must be antecedent, that is, the marriage must result from the fear. A mere concomitant fear, if it is not also the cause of the marriage, does not result in invalidity for the marriage.[64] Again, the fear would not be an invalidating cause if the affected party could free himself from

[58] For the same argument, but involving a different case, cf. c. 17, X, *de sponsalibus et matrimoniis,* IV, 1: *"quum actiones huiusmodi difficiles soleant exitus frequenter habere."*

[59] Woywod-Smith, *Commentary,* I, 656. Cf. Reg. 27, R. J., in VI°: *Scienti et consentienti non fit iniuria neque dolus."* For a discussion of the point, cf. Reiffenstuel, *Tractatus de Regulis Juris* (Ingolstadii, 1733), Cap. II, Reg. 27, n. 8.

[60] *De Matrimonio,* n. 607.

[61] *De Matrimonio,* II, n. 1685, (2).

[62] *Theologiae Moralis Principia—Responsa—Consilia* (4 vols., Brugis, Vol. I, 2. ed., 1926; Vol. II, 2. ed., 1928; Vol. III, 1923; Vol. IV, 2. ed., 1926), III, n. 789 (b) (hereafter cited *Theologia Moralis*).

[63] Obviously the reference is to canon 1017, § 3, which denies the right of action to force a party to contract marriage, though that party refuses to fulfill a canonically valid promise of marriage.

[64] Coronata, *De Matrimonio,* n. 479.

the compulsion, and escape the threatened evil without serious difficulty in some other way than by marriage.[65]

Formerly there had been a controversy whether the coercion had to relate to the contracting of marriage with a determined person, or simply to the contracting of marriage in general. That the latter case also reflects the presence of an invalidating fear is held as certain by Cappello, who bases his statement on the "wording of the Code and the very end of the law."[66]

But there is another controversy which has not been settled. Before the promulgation of the Code it was quite generally held that the fear had to be inflicted directly for the purpose of coercing the matrimonial consent. But many post-Code canonists hold that a fear indirectly inflicted for that purpose suffices to invalidate a given marriage. The shift of opinion is occasioned by the wording of canon 1087, § 1, *"a quo ut quis se liberet, eligere cogatur matrimonium"* which is used instead of the classical phrase, *"ad extorquendum matrimonium."*

In the following discussion of the controversy the divergent opinions will be designated as the restrictive theory and the inclusive theory. The *restrictive theory* points to the opinion which holds that only a directly inflicted fear will invalidate the marriage; the *inclusive theory* connotes the doctrine which proposes that an indirectly as well as a directly inflicted fear will invalidate the marriage.

The restrictive opinion was held, e. g., by Sanchez (1550-1610),[67] Reiffenstuel (1642-1703),[68] and Wernz (1842-1914).[69] The directly inflicted fear was referred to as *metus directus, metus directe incussus, metus consultus,* and *metus consulto incussus.* These expressions indicated that for the invalidation of the marriage the threatened evil as the cause of the fear had to be motivated directly (*directe*) or specifically (*consulto*) by the intent or purpose of forcing the contracting of the marriage.

The fundamental argument of those who maintained this re-

---

[65] *Decisiones,* XXVI (1934), 772; Coronata, *De Matrimonio,* n. 479; Cappello, *De Matrimonio,* n. 607.

[66] *De Matrimonio,* n. 607; *Decisiones,* XXVII (1935), 71.

[67] *De Matrimonii Sacramento,* Lib. IV, disp. XII, n. 3.

[68] Lib. IV, tit. 1, n. 328.

[69] *Ius Matrimoniale,* n. 265, note 25.

strictive opinion was that a compulsion for the contracting of marriage existed only when the fear was unjustly inflicted for that very purpose, and that, if the fear was inflicted apart from this direct intent, then also it was not employed for the purpose of forcing the victim to contract the marriage; the inflicted fear thus became the occasion, and not the cause, for the victim's contracting of marriage. Gasparri illustrated this kind of inflicted fear with the following example: a father threatens to kill his daughter's seducer because of the latter's criminal action, but his act of threat is not motivated with any intention of forcing him to marry her.[70]

Some Post-Code authors still propose this restrictive theory, for they claim that the wording as contained in the present Code has not affected the continued tenableness of the pre-Code restrictive theory. Payen, for instance, held this,[71] and he quoted with approval the argument of Wernz[72] that an inflicted fear which abstracted from the enforced contracting of marriage as its direct purpose existed not as an efficacious cause, but simply as an *occasion* by which the affected party himself made the decision, through an act of free choice, for the exchanging of the matrimonial consent. Several other authors still maintain this opinion.[73]

The other opinion, here termed the inclusive theory, which maintained that an indirectly inflicted fear could likewise invalidate marriage, was propounded before the Code, particularly by Schmalzgrueber (1663-1735).[74]

Since 1918 several authors have adopted this inclusive theory, for they hold that it is justified by the wording of canon 1087, § 1, as representing a change from the restrictive sense of the classical phrase *"ad extorquendum matrimonium."* Their chief

---

70 *De Matrimonio,* n. 856.

71 *De Matrimonio,* II, n. 1686, (2).

72 *Ius Matrimoniale,* n. 265, note 25.

73 E. g., Vidal, *Ius Matrimoniale,* n. 501 with note 27; Genicot-Salsmans, *Institutiones,* II, n. 463, 4°; Lega-Bartoccetti, *Commentarius in Iudicia Ecclesiastica iuxta Codicem Iuris Canonici* (3 vols., Vols. I, II, Anonima Libraria Cattolica Italiana, 1938-1939; Vol. III, Editiones Comm. A. Arnodo, 1941: Romae), I, 425 (hereafter cited *Commentarius*).

74 *Jus Ecclesiasticum Universum* (5 vols. in 12, Romae, 1843-1845), Lib. IV, tit. 1, n. 399.

argument is that, even though the one who employs the fear does not directly propose to achieve the coercing of the marriage, yet if there is no other way of freeing oneself from the impact of that fear than through the contracting of marriage, the fear really exists as a cause which induces the contracting of the marriage. If the fear was at the same time grave and inflicted by a human agent unjustly, then the marriage which was contracted in consequence of it was to be regarded as invalid. The foundation for this argument is that the law considers the attitude of the affected party, inasmuch as he unwillingly adopts the choice of marriage, rather than the attitude of the party who when inflicting the fear did not directly demand the contracting of marriage. The party inflicting the fear has indeed not specificially indicated the contracting of marriage as the only alternative, but in effect the victim of the fear is in his own mind still confronted with but a single choice as an inseparable consequence of the unjustly inflicted fear. In protecting the free and unhampered approach in the contracting of marriage, the Church proceeds from the viewpoint of the party contracting the marriage, and not from that of the party inflicting the fear.[75]

A number of post-Code authors maintain that this inclusive theory can be accepted as certain in principle, and that at any rate it is to be accepted as certain in practice.[76] They usually refer to the specific data given by Gasparri and Roberti on the change of the pre-Code terminology. Gasparri noted that in the preparation of the Code the first draft of canon 1087 used the phrase *ad extorquendum consensum matrimonialem,* which favored

---

[75] Cappello, *De Matrimonio,* n. 607; Roberti, *De Processibus,* I, n. 259; Coronata, *De Matrimonio,* n. 479.

[76] Coronata: *"certo videtur"*—*De Matrimonio,* n. 479; Cappello: *"id liquet"* —*De Matrimonio,* n. 607; Roberti: *"evidenter"*—*De Processibus,* n. 259; Gasparri: *"satis apparet"*—*De Matrimonio,* n. 857; Vermeersch-Creusen: *"disputationi locus iam non est"*—*Epitome,* II, 376; Doheny: (implicitly)—*Canonical Procedure in Matrimonial Cases* (2 vols., Vol. I, 2. ed., 1948; Vol. II, 1944, Milwaukee: Bruce), I, p. 902 (hereafter Vol. I cited as *Formal Procedure* and Vol. II as *Informal Procedure;* Bouscaren-Ellis: "seems certainly correct"—*Canon Law, A Text and Commentary* (Milwaukee: Bruce, 1946), p. 509 (hereafter cited *Commentary*); Chelodi-Ciprotti: *"controversiae . . . definitive sublatae videntur"*—*De Matrimonio,* n. 119.

the restrictive opinion.[77] After some discussion, the suggestion of Palmieri (1829-1909) was followed. He had suggested the use of the phrase now found in the canon, *"a quo ut quis se liberet, eligere cogatur matrimonium."* It was then understood that the wording would leave room for the application of the inclusive as well as the restrictive theory. So Gasparri stated on the same page that a marriage would be invalid even if the inflicted fear was not a directly inflicted fear.

Roberti mentions that Lega (1860-1935), (Cardinal in 1914), considered that the words *ex metu gravi et iniuste incusso* signified that the fear had to be directed toward the coercion of consent, but that Ojetti denied this, and hoped that the question concerning the motivation of the fear might be *left open to discussion by the doctors,* since he thought that any grave fear, whether direct or indirect in its influence, could suffice for the invalidation of an act.[78]

However, it must be noted that this difference of opinion was specifically connected with canon 1684, § 1, of the present Code, where a contract is left open to a possible recission if it was sealed under the influence of a grave fear unjustly inflicted upon either or both of the contracting parties. But marriage is not a recissible contract, and hence the analogy that may exist between canons 1087 and 1684 must be utilized most cautiously. Furthermore, since there *was* a difference of opinion, a definitive unanimity in the mind of the codifiers just mentioned is not necessarily reflected in the final wording of the Code, even though in accordance with the norm of canon 18 one may feel necessitated to look to the mind of the legislator for the proper sense and understanding of the specific legislation here in question.

Payen, in disagreeing with Gasparri, stated that we must distinguish between the intent of the writers of the Code and the expression of this intent.[79] He admitted that Gasparri has given

---

[77] Gasparri, *De Matrimonio,* n. 856.

[78] Roberti, *Codicis Iuris Canonici Schemata,* Lib. IV: *De Processibus,* I: *De Iudiciis in Genere* (In Civitate Vaticana: Typis Polyglottis Vaticanis, 1940), Schema D, Can. 167, note 13 (pp. 176-177).—Canon 167 here corresponds to canon 1684, § 1, of the present Code. Cf. Roberti, *De Processibus,* n. 259 (p. 694, note 8).

[79] Payen, *De Matrimonio,* II, n. 1686 (p. 85), note 6.

us the intent of the writers, but he also claimed that the actual wording of the law has not taken away all doubt. This is borne out by the fact that other authors besides Payen still hold to the restrictive theory.[80]

However, the shift to the inclusive theory is represented by a good number of authors, as indicated above. The Rota has also gradually accepted this doctrine, although it is understandable that the Rota has not made frequent references to it inasmuch as cases which involve solely an indirect fear are of extremely rare occurrence. Actually, it seems that no specific case of this type has come before the Rota. But some references have been made in Rota decisions to the inclusive theory. They are to be found in the *In iure* statements of principles. It is to be noted that the references which will be quoted were only statements of theory, and did not serve directly in the settlement of the causes which were under discussion before the Rota.

In 1922, a Rota decision carried this statement: "It makes no difference whether the fear influences the matrimonial consent directly or indirectly."[81] In a decision given in 1933, the Rota stated the following: "Hence by the law of the Code a marriage is invalid not only if the grave fear has been inflicted directly with a view to compelling a matrimonial consent, but also if it has been inflicted not directly for this purpose, but the party is nevertheless convinced that he cannot free himself from the fear unless he contracts marriage." The decision continued by citing Gasparri and referring to the special weight of his opinion in view of his being the head of the commission that edited the Code. The decision stated that the Code "wished to settle and therefore has settled the controversy among canonists on this point," and that "in consequence of the absence of any likely error the tribunals must feel obliged to follow the new formula, as it has been explained above."[82]

Again, in 1937, a Rota decision held: "For an evil to give rise to an invalidating fear . . . a connection must intervene be-

---

[80] E. g., Wernz-Vidal, as edited by P. Aguirre in 1946, *Ius Matrimoniale*, n. 501, and note 27; Lega-Bartoccetti, as edited by Bartoccetti in 1938, *Commentarius*, I, 425.

[81] *Decisiones*, XIV (1922), 3.

[82] *Decisiones*, XXV (1933), 608-609.

tween that evil and the marriage which on account of it is contracted, whether the fear of the evil is directly inflicted for the coercing of the consent, or whether 'the party is convinced that he cannot free himself from the fear of this evil unless he contracts marriage' (Gasparri, *De matr.*, ed. 1932, II, n. 856)."[83]

Roberti observed (in his 1941 edition) that jurisprudence on the point was uncertain in the first few years after the Code, but that in later years there has been a strong shift to adopt the inclusive theory.[84] He cited a Rota case[85] which quoted Gasparri[86] almost verbatim, and which clearly accepted Gasparri's doctrine, in accord with the inclusive theory, that also an indirectly inflicted grave fear suffices to invalidate the marriage. Besides referring to this case, Robert adds, *"et pluries,"* indicating that several other decisions contain this doctrine. The writer was able to find only two other decisions in the same volume that clearly and explicitly held the same doctrine.[87] In the four preceding volumes no clear and unmistakable statement of the doctrine could be found.[88]

But for the same period (1934-1938 inclusive) there were decisions which more or less explicitly held the opposite opinion.[89]

However, one may say that these examples do not explicitly state that an indirectly inflicted fear cannot invalidate the marriage; there is simply a strong insistence that a directly inflicted fear can, and, if it is grave does, invalidate the marriage contracted because of it.

---

83 *Decisiones,* XXIX (1937), 783.

84 *De Processibus,* I, n. 259 (p. 695), note 1.

85 *Decisiones,* XXX (1938), 251.

86 *De Matrimonio,* n. 856.

87 *Decisiones,* XXX (1938), 438, 650. Other decisions that seem to hint at the doctrine can be found on pp. 370, 417, 641.

88 *Decisiones,* XXVI-XXIX (1934-1937). As an example of apparent adherence to the inclusive theory: "Therefore, to show that marriage is invalid on the head of force and fear, it is necessary to prove that a grave, extrinsic, and unjust evil, which could not be avoided except by marriage, threatened one of the parties."—*Decisiones,* XXVI (1934), 719. The Rota here does not distinguish between direct and indirect threat of the evil.

89 The following examples may suffice. "And inflicted, moreover, to the end that the one undergoing the fear should celebrate some marriage."—*Decisiones,* XXVI (1934), 257. "The same is verified [that marriage was

The following solution for the controversy is offered under the following five heads: 1) the arguments from Roberti; 2) emphasis on the notion of fear; 3) change of formula; 4) indentification of indirect with direct fear; 5) the extremely rare case.

A. *The Arguments from Roberti*

Roberti presents a series of arguments for the inclusive theory.[90] He notes the two general arguments for the restrictive theory (which he calls the *consulto* theory), as taken from Sanchez. The first of these contends that by indirect fear a man is not impelled to the juridical act, but acts spontaneously; the second, that the involuntariness in the juridical act does not derive from the intention of the one inflicting the fear, but rather from the evil which occasions the fear.

In defense of the inclusive (*etiam inconsulto*) theory Roberti offers the following arguments (here summarized). Force is present, for the one affected by the fear must choose between either an act of resistance, or an act of toleration, relative to the evil or evils threatened. Granted that the threatened evils are grave, the will is really coerced by means of a grave evil. There is truly present the infliction of an injury, for it can be said that virtually the suffered fear impels its victim to perform the act whereby an escape from the unjustly threatened evil be effected. If the victim chooses what appears to him as the lesser of the two evils, one cannot in consequence conclude that the inflicted injury has thereby become neutralized.

In specific application to marriage, Roberti lists five reasons (here summarized).

---

not *caused* by injustice, and hence not by injury] if the fear was not inflicted with the intention that some marriage be celebrated. The marriage to be celebrated does not depend on and does not result from the fear, when the connection between the two has been removed."—*Decisiones,* XXVI (1934), 765. "And of design [*consultus*], that is, in order to force the giving of marriage consent."—*Decisiones,* XXVII (1935), 213. "And directed toward forcing the giving of matrimonial consent."—*Decisiones,* XXX (1938), 429. "And with reference to [*intuitu*] the celebration of marriage."—*Decisiones,* XXX (1938), 3.

90 "De metu indirecto quoad negotia iuridica praesertim matrimonium," *Apollinaris* (Romae, 1928—), XI (1938), 557-561.

1. No canonical norm postulates that the fear must have been inflicted directly with a view to compelling the expression of matrimonial consent.

2. On the score of the nature of fear itself, the direct infliction of it is not a prerequisite condition. The fear is to be considered as it exists in the victim whose freedom of choice is being restricted by that fear. This restriction can derive from an indirectly as well as a directly employed threat of evil, for in either contingency the contracting of marriage may appear as the only means of escaping the fear.

3. The purpose of the one who inflicts the fear is indeed not precisely that of intimidating the will of the party. But the intimidation which has resulted nonetheless exists as an unjustly sustained injury, whether the inflicted fear was of direct or indirect intent.

4. Fear can derive from an extrinsic source whether it has been inflicted directly or indirectly. An act placed because of indirect fear is an *involuntarium secundum quid,* and is to be attributed to the causality of the human agent acting *ab extrinseco,* and not to any spontaneous choice of the party affected.

5. Even by means of an indirectly instilled fear the victim is truly forced to choose marriage. The root of the vitiation of the consent lies in the affected party. The threatening party has unjustly inflicted the fear, directly or indirectly, and this fear moves the affected party to give consent under duress.

B. *Emphasis on the Notion of Fear*

The old phrase, *ad extorquendum consensum,* is more easily interpreted as referring to direct fear only, and most of the pre-Code authors took this view. The phrase emphasized the *forcing* of the consent. But the new wording of the Code emphasizes the notion of *fear: a quo ut quis se liberet, eligere cogatur matrimonium.* If the fear impels the party to choose marriage as a sole means for escaping the fear, it falls under the meaning of the canon. No mention occurs regarding the precise intention of the one who inflicts the fear, namely, whether he proposes or abstracts from the enforced expression of matrimonial consent. Hence an indirect instilling of fear can suffice for the invalidation of the consent expressed in consequence of being victimized by that fear.

C. *Change of Formula*

A changed wording in the law may reflect the desire of clarifying the meaning of the law. This in turn can involve the rejection of some previous interpretation on the point at issue. The point here at issue involves the two opposite opinions, the restrictive and the inclusive theories. The restrictive theory seemed favored by the old wording. Little if any advantage would have derived from a change in that wording if the pre-Code restrictive theory was to be maintained, unless perhaps the legislator had expressly used the phrase *et directe incussum.* However, on the supposition that the Code intended to favor the inclusive opinion, the insertion of such a phrase as *directe vel indirecte incussum* would have demanded a further and explicit explanation, since such a phrase would also have related to cases of indirect fear in which the contracting of marriage was not regarded by the victim as the sole available means of escaping the threatened evil.[91]

For this reason Cappello adds the following caution: "It is entirely necessary that in such a hypothesis [the invalidating effect of the indirectly inflicted fear] the choice of marriage, whether in itself or in consequence of circumstances, be the necessary and generally also the only means of setting aside the fear; otherwise the true coercion which invalidates the marriage does not obtain in the case.[92] Hence an entirely new phrase which in its substitution for the older phrase can hardly be alleged as *strengthening* the restrictive theory seems rather to have the effect of negating it, and of adopting in place of it the only alternative, the inclusive theory.

---

[91] Wyszynski, "Utrum metus indirecte incussus dirimere possit matrimonium,"—*Jus Pontificium,* XIII (1933), 62. The entire 46-page article is distributed in the *Jus Pontificium,* X (1930), 193-200; XI (1931), 42-51; XII (1932), 43-52, 122-127; XIII (1933), 52-63. It is also published in brochure form in the series, *Dissertationes ex Ephemeridibus JUS PONTIFICIUM excerptae ac separatim editae* (Romae: *Jus Pontificium,* 1933), Series II, Fasc. XX; the corresponding citation in this brochure is p. 45. The article gives historical and textual arguments for the inclusive theory.

[92] *De Matrimonio,* n. 607; Wyszynski, *Jus Pontificium, loc. cit.*

Payen argued that the word *"cogatur"* in canon 1087, § 1, points to the kind of fear that was directly inflicted for the purpose of compelling the exchange of a matrimonial consent.[93] But the canon does not characterize the intention of the one inflicting the fear. It abstracts from the fact whether or not the instilled fear was employed for the purpose of compelling the expression of a matrimonial consent. On the contrary, the canon emphasizes the notion of fear (as has been noted above) that leads to the contracting of the marriage. Once the fear is inflicted by a human agent, it becomes also a fear that impels the affected party, whatever the intention of the inflicting agent may have been.

D. *Identification of Indirect with Direct Fear*

No one doubts that cases accompanied with only the element of indirect fear are indeed rare. If a case of this type should occur, there could easily arise some doubt whether the intention to compel the exchange of marriage consent was actually absent. If a positive doubt did arise, the presumption would rather point to the presence of a direct fear. In practice it would be very nearly impossible to prove that a direct fear was not simultaneously involved along with an indirect fear.[94]

This leads to a discussion of the three examples of indirect fear as given by Gasparri.[95] They are the following: 1) Titius makes a murderous attack upon Caia, so she offers marriage in order to escape death, and Titius accepts; 2) The father intends to kill Titius, the seducer of his daughter Anna; Titius, to save himself, suggests marriage with Anna, and the father agrees; 3) When a physician, from hatred or laziness or for some other reason, refuses to give to a sick woman the treatment that in due justice and by reason of his office he is bound to bestow upon her; the woman promises to marry him or his son. In all three cases the logical steps are the same; the aggressor makes a threat without reference to marriage, the one threatened offers marriage, the aggressor accepts. For the purpose of discussion, the second example can serve for all three.

---

93 *De Matrimonio,* II, n. 1686, (2), note 6.

94 Reiffenstuel, Lib. I, tit. 40, n. 29.

95 *De Matrimonio,* n. 856.

The example, as far as it goes, involves only indirect fear. But between the acceptance by the agressor, and the actual time of the celebration of marriage, there is an interim, however short it may be. During this interim, so it appears, the inflicted fear takes on a new characteristic. Once the father, the aggressor, has accepted the proposal of marriage, he has implicitly agreed that the victim of his threat *now* has the choice of the two alternatives, death or marriage. If he has agreed explicitly, the case is all the more obviously one of direct fear. But though the father may have agreed only implicitly, the threat is thereupon effectively directed toward forcing the giving of a marriage consent. The *agreement* to marry is extorted indeed through the use of indirect fear, but after this agreement the forced marriage consent will ensue as the result of a directly inflicted fear under a new implied agreement: "From *now on* it is a question of marriage or death." This supposes that the threat of death is still intended as an effective threat. Otherwise the seducer could, without the sustaining of a grave fear, refuse to marry. But the aggressor needs to have neutralized the fear effectively and unconditionally, thus leaving the seducer free to enter or to forego the marriage.

This conclusion, different from Gasparri's[96] is then offered: an agreement to marry may indeed be caused by even an indirect fear, but once the agreement is made, then the fear is also directly inflicted with a view to forcefully obtaining from the victim his or her expression of matrimonial consent.

E) *The Extremely Rare Case*

Granted the existence of the extremely rare case in which the indirect fear has not become transformed into a direct fear, it seems that a declaration of nullity would not be warranted for the marriage in question. There is at least sound extrinsic probability for this restrictive opinion. A few authors, fairly recent in their statements, still held that theory. Furthermore, some very recent decisions of the Rota are by no means clearly in favor of the inclusive theory. The controversy is not by any means absolutely settled, and so the presumption of law, as determined in

---

[96] *De Matrimonio*, n. 856.

canon 1014, will continue to favor the validity of the marriage, unless the Holy See adopts as undoubted and indisputable the principle that the presence of an indirect grave fear calls for a declaration of nullity.[97]

Article 3. Exclusion of Other Types of Fear

Canon 1087, § 2: No other fear entails the nullity of marriage though it caused the contract to be made.[98]

This is more or less a re-statement of the first paragraph of the same canon. It emphasizes, in its negative form, the exclusion of types of fear that do not satisfy the conditions postulated in the first paragraph. Hence invalidity for a marriage cannot result from grave fear that is just, from intrinsic fear, and especially from slight fear, even though it constituted the very reason for entering the marriage.[99]

Two former controversies were definitely settled by the principle of law enunciated in this canon. One controversy dealt with the question whether a grave fear *justly* inflicted invalidated the marriage. The affirmative opinion had few proponents, and the negative opinion was held to be certain even long before the promulgation of the Code.[100]

The second controversy centered on the question whether a slight fear invalidated the marriage in the event that it served as a cause for the contract. De Lugo (1583-1660) was probably the last to hold the affirmative opinion.[101]

At any rate the controversies were settled by the principle of law

---

[97] Vromant, *Ius Missionariorum*, Tomus V, *De Matrimonio* (Louvain: Museum Lessianum, 1931), n. 190 (hereafter cited *De Matrimonio*).

[98] Translation from Woywod-Smith, *Commentary*, I, 655.

[99] Cappello, *De Matrimonio*, n. 607; Doheny, *Formal Procedure*, p. 903.

[100] Sanchez mentioned the affirmative opinion and admitted that it was probable, but himself maintained the negative opinion.—*De Matrimonii Sacramento*, Lib. IV, disp. 13, n. 3. Later, Reiffenstuel stated that the negative opinion reflected the common and certain doctrine, and in one place did not even mention the opposite opinion,—Lib. IV, tit. 1, n. 329; in another place he merely remarked, "although some hold the opposite."—Lib. I, tit. 40, n. 27. Wernz, in his discussion of the natural law theory, rejected the idea that a just fear could invalidate the marriage.—*Ius Matrimoniale*, n. 266.

[101] *Disputationes de Iustitia et Iure* (2. ed., 2 vols., in 1, Venetiis, 1751), disp. XXII, n. 141. Sanchez gave a list of those who held the affirmative

now expressed in canon 1087, § 2. The clause, *"etiamsi det causam contractui"* may be considered as furnishing the very marrow inherent in the strong exclusion of the erstwhile supported doctrine that a slight fear which gave rise to the contract sufficed for the invalidation of the marriage. Other than this the second paragraph of the canon merely emphasizes the positive statement of the first paragraph, as was indicated at the beginning of this article.

Invalidity of the marriage on account of fear pertains of necessity to both forums, the internal and the external.[102] Whenever there is a doubt, so that the fear sustained in the making of the contract cannot be established as having been invalidating in its character, the marriage, for the simple reason that it enjoys the favor of the law, must be held as valid.[103] Schmalzgrueber offered and discussed the opinion that it would be better to declare a marriage invalid when its validity was doubtful on account of the accompanying element of fear,[104] but he finally rejected it for the reason that the presumption must stand for the validity of the marriage.[105]

Cappello, in discussing the same point, quotes Schmalzgrueber at length, and substantially furnishes the same analysis that has just been indicated. He also notes that in a doubt of fact (e. g., concerning the gravity of the fear) the marriage must be considered valid. But with reference to a doubt of law (e. g., whether reverential fear combined with importunate pleas can invalidate the marriage) he sees room for controversy. Notwithstanding the acknowledged possibility for a controversy, he considers it by far the more probable opinion that in principle the marriage in question is to be upheld as valid, and that in practice it cannot be declared as invalid.[106]

---

opinion during his time, and he still called it a probable opinion, though he admitted the negative opinion as the more probable one.—*De Matrimonii Sacramento,* Lib. IV, disp. XVII, nn. 2, 4. Wernz rejected the slight fear theory entirely.—*Ius Matrimoniale,* n. 263.

102 Coronata, *De Matrimonio,* n. 479; Gasparri, *De Matrimonio,* n. 851.

103 Cappello, *De Matrimonio,* n. 607, *in fin.;* canon 1014.

104 Lib. IV, tit. 1, n. 401.

105 Lib. IV, tit. 1, n. 432; Chelodi-Ciprotti, *De Matrimonio,* n. 7.

106 Cappello, *De Matrimonio,* n. 55.

CHAPTER II

NATURAL LAW ON FEAR

ARTICLE 1. THE CONTROVERSY

Since the Middle Ages there has been a controversy, apparently insoluble, dealing with the question of the origin of the invalidating effect of fear that affects marriage consent. The controversy hinges on the point whether grave and at the same time unjustly inflicted fear, when it does not wholly neutralize consent but nevertheless diminishes its freedom, derives its nullifying force immediately from the natural law or solely and entirely from positive law.[1]

There is no doubt that a marriage extorted by absolute physical force is invalid by the natural law.[2] Similarly, if fear rendered the use of reason completely inoperative, the marriage would be invalid by the natural law.[3] In either case the explanation is obvious: no consent was given, and marriage is contracted only by consent.[4]

In the controversy it is generally admitted that the natural law furnishes congruous reasons for the positive law's recognition and enactment that a notably diminished measure of consent constitutes a hindrance to a valid marriage. Again, there is a general admission on the part of the authors that the extent of this hindrance is not precisely determined in the natural law, so that it remains for the positive law to indicate just how comprehensive in scope this hindrance is. The controversy quite generally centers around the substantial elements of this hindrance.[5]

The controversy is apparently insoluble, since none of the reasons given on either side are thoroughly conclusive. The authors

---

[1] Sangmeister, *Force and Fear,* p. 154. Sangmeister here uses the expression ecclesiastical law instead of positive law. But the controversy can also be referred to infidels, and in their marriages the positive civil law is also involved. Positive law would then seem the better expression here.

[2] Sangmeister, *Force and Fear,* p. 154.

[3] Coronata, *De Matrimonio,* n. 480; Gasparri, *De Matrimonio,* n. 833.

[4] Wernz-Vidal, *De Matrimonio,* n. 503.

[5] Coronata, *De Matrimonio,* n. 480.

ranged on each side are about equal in number and authority. This fairly even division can be found in any period.[6]

Article 2. Comparison of the Theories

The arguments proposed by the two sides are in almost perfect antithesis. Each argument is met with a counter-argument on the same general grounds. For this reason, as each argument for the natural law theory is given, the counter-argument from the positive law theory will be immediately supplied. Only a few of the arguments will here be given some closer consideration, since many of the arguments listed in various works are of minor import. The arguments will be grouped under three headings: a) natural equity; b) comparison of fear and fraud; c) documents.

a) natural equity

Perhaps the principal argument in favor of the natural law theory is that which is drawn from the concept of natural equity. Natural equity demands that the person who is forced into marriage by means of a moral coercion should have his rights vindicated through a restoration to him of his prior status. In other contracts the person is protected through the rescissible character of the contract. But such a protection cannot be given in the case of Christian marriage for the simple reason that it is a contract of indissoluble character.[7] The innocent party would be forced into a life made intolerable by obligations which were not voluntarily assumed. The party guilty of inflicting the fear would gain a distinct advantage and profit from his injustice. The rightful possibility of such an outcome would be repugnant to the natural law. Hence the natural law must make provision for the interests of justice through the only means available, that is, the invalidity of the marriage from the beginning.[8]

Those who support the positive law theory make these objec-

---

[6] Sangmeister lists 17 authors favoring the natural law theory (*Force and Fear*, p. 155, note 5), and 19 authors favoring the positive law theory (*op. cit.*, p. 157, note 15).

[7] Coronata, *De Matrimonio*, n. 480; Reiffenstuel, Lib. IV, tit. 1, n. 325.

[8] St. Thomas, *Summa Theologica, Suppl.*, q. 47, a. 3; Sangmeister, *Force and Fear*, pp. 155-156; Payen, *De Matrimonio*, II, n. 1689.

tions. Fear, even though it is grave and unjust, does not invalidate other contracts. If it is held that fear does invalidate marriage, it is not sufficiently clear that only *unjust fear* invalidates marriage.[9]

In reply to the objection that fear does not invalidate other contracts, the natural law theory maintains that this is precisely the reason for insisting that it invalidates the contract of marriage, since the contract of marriage does not allow of a rescinding as a means for protecting natural equity. In reply to the objection that other types of fear are not excluded in a sufficiently and satisfactorily discriminating manner, the natural law theory claims that natural equity does exclude them. This is so because the presence of an intrinsic natural or supernatural fear does not involve the infliction of any injury. Whatever moral force is reflected in the circumstances is there as something for which the party himself is answerable.[10]

To the objection that slight fear would also invalidate marriage by the natural law, the reply may be made that natural equity does not urge such a postulate, since a person who possesses a reasonable measure of resoluteness (*vir constans*) will not yield to the contracting of marriage under the provocation of a slight fear. His ready defense against possible injury consists in his reasoned appraisal that marriage is too important a consideration to yield place to the influence of a slight fear. The very notion of a slight fear implies that it can be overcome by a reasonably resolute person. From every injury which a slight fear may have caused there is a ready escape by means of a normally resolute act which can be easily enough achieved by any resolute person.[11]

b) COMPARISON OF FEAR AND FRAUD

Against the natural law theory there is raised the objection which claims that this theory must then with equal reason admit that fraud (even though substantial error is not involved) should also invalidate marriage. Yet, so it is urged, from the close circumscription which canon 1083 reflects, it is obvious that some

---

9 Juarez, *Vis et Metus,* p. 44; Gasparri, *De Matrimonio,* n. 841.

10 Coronata, *De Matrimonio,* n. 480.

11 Wernz-Vidal, *Ius Matrimoniale,* n. 499.

types of error and fraud do not invalidate marriage. This objection was raised even before the promulgation of the Code.[12]

In countering this objection, the natural law theory claims that the argument is based on an imperfect parity between fear and fraud. This is so because fraud directly affects the intellect, while fear immediately and intrinsically moves the will.[13] As long as the case of substantial error is precluded, fraud is something which exists antecedently and by way of occasion. The deceived party enters the contract willingly, so that the defect lies entirely in the antecedent error which furnished an occasion for the giving of the consent. Fear, however, not only impels a person intrinsically to give his consent, but vitiates the consent itself by keeping it intrinsically deficient. The quasi-unwillingness thus involved clashes with the idea of a voluntary and free action of the will. In consequence of this the (natural) law plays the role of a more intensive guardian for the one who succumbs to fear than for the one who is subjected to fraud.[14]

This analysis is countered quite tersely with the observation that a grave but at the same time just fear likewise entails a defective freedom for consent; logically, then, a grave but simultaneously just fear should also invalidate any marriage contracted under its influence.[15] In reply the natural law theory argues that both a just fear and one which proceeds from within are not of the same character as the fear which derives from without through its unjust infliction by a free agent, and that to claim the same juridical effects for the various types of fear is to argue upon a false basis of parity.[16]

c) DOCUMENTS

Official documents do not furnish conclusive proofs for either side. The wording is usually open to various interpretations. An Instruction dealing with the impediment of abduction is usually cited for the natural law theory: "*Impedimentum . . . alterum*

---

[12] Schmalzgrueber, Lib. IV, tit. 1, n. 407, ad 5.

[13] Wernz-Vidal, *Ius Matrimoniale,* n. 502.

[14] De Lugo, *Disputationes de Iustitia et Iure,* disp. XXII, n. 173.

[15] Juarez, *Vis et Metus,* p. 47.

[16] Wernz-Vidal, *Ius Matrimoniale,* n. 502; Payen, *De Matrimonio,* II, n. 1689, (2).

scilicet . . . ex capite vis et metus, quod reapse consensum afficit quodque proinde in ipso iure naturali fundamentum habet; . . . quoties adsit, nullus dispensationi sit locus."[17] At best this passage can be considered as a guarded, though somewhat approving reference to the natural law theory.[18] But some writers claim that it can just as easily be interpreted to mean that the natural law simply furnishes a basis for the impediment, but that formally the impediment derives its existence from the positive law only.[19]

Rota decisions do not attempt to take sides in the controversy. In their occasional references to the two theories they leave the question open. This is the case even in recent decisions.[20] A very recent decision referred to the natural law theory in this guarded wording: "Consent, which makes marriage, must be free from coercion on the part of the will. This is required by the very law of nature, but it is only the positive ecclesiastical law that more accurately determines the conditions under which the defect of liberty in the one contracting can have invalidating force."[21]

There is no need to multiply quotations from documents. The wording is always so guarded that either side can find an interpretation in its own favor.

CONCLUSION

From a consideration of the two theories as here discussed it seems that the natural law theory offers the greater probability for correctness. The principal reason for holding this rests in the argument which is drawn from the concept of natural equity. Although open to strong objections, this argument seems to evince that the invalidating effect of fear, if it be a grave fear unjustly

---

[17] S. C. S. Off., instr., 15 febr., 1901—*Fontes,* IV, 1250.

[18] Wernz-Vidal (*Ius Matrimoniale,* n. 502) claims no more than: "hisce verbis *insinuatur.*"

[19] Jaurez, *Vis et Metus,* p. 48; Sangmeister, *Force and Fear,* pp. 162-163; Gasparri, *De Matrimonio,* n. 841.

[20] *Decisiones,* XXVI (1934), 49: "There are some who derive this impediment from the very law of nature"; *Decisiones,* XXVI (1934), 664; "There are some canonists who derive this impediment from the natural law itself."

[21] *Decisiones,* XXXI (1939), 149.

inflicted, is substantially identified as part and parcel of the natural law, rather than as something which only strikes root in the natural law. This conclusion will have a practical bearing on two points that will now be considered: dispensation, and the marriages of infidels and of non-Catholics.

Article 3. Dispensation

From the natural law theory it follows that the faithful and the infidels alike invalidly contract marriage if they are impelled to do so by a fear that is grave, unjust and inflicted from without. Furthermore, the Church could not dispense either the faithful or the infidels in this matter, whether for the purpose of contracting a marriage or of convalidating a marriage.[22]

According to the positive law theory, the Church would inherently and fundamentally possess the power of dispensing the faithful, but because of the doubt regarding the natural law on the matter does not dispense.[23]

As long as the controversy continues, it is easily understood why the Church never dispenses, not even after an invalid marriage had been contracted. In the first place, it is doubtful whether a dispensation can be given. Until the controversy is definitely settled, a doubt of law, divine or positive, exists. For this reason the power of the Pope to dispense from the law remains in question. If, despite this doubt, a dispensation were to be granted, he would expose himself to the danger of violating the natural law from which he cannot dispense.[24]

Secondly, even granted that the positive law theory were established, the Church would hardly remove the nullity by dispensing from the law. The nullity is enacted as a protection for the party who has suffered compulsion, and a dispensation would entirely remove the protection the party needs in order not to become obligated under an unwanted contract. Again, by dispensation, the person responsible for the injustice would gain a distinct advantage from his malicious action. *Metum comprobare contra*

[22] Cf. Coronata, *De Matrimonio,* n. 480.

[23] Coronata, *De Matrimonio,* n. 480.

[24] Sangmeister, *Force and Fear,* pp. 165-166; Wernz-Vidal, *Ius Matrimoniale,* n. 503.

bonos mores est.[25] This alone would be a sufficient reason for never giving the dispensation.[26] The Holy Office stated the doctrine clearly: *"Impedimentum . . . scilicet ex capite vis et metus, quod reapse consensum afficit quodque proinde in ipso iure naturali fundamentum habet: . . . quoties adsit, nullus dispensationi sit locus."*[27]

Article 4. The Marriages of Infidels and of non-Catholics

The natural law controversy has a direct bearing on the marriages of infidels and of non-Catholics that were contracted under the influence of a grave, unjust, and extrinsic fear. Granted that the natural law theory is correct, such marriages would be invalid, independently of the existence of any positive law governing the matter.

In order to discuss the question in detail, the matter will be grouped under three heads: a) marriages of infidels with infidels; b) marriages of infidels with baptized parties; c) marriages between two baptized parties.

Section 1. Marriages of Infidels with Infidels

According to the natural law theory, a marriage between two infidels contracted under the influence of a grave, unjust and inflicted fear is invalid in virtue of the natural law, whether one or both of the parties were under the influence of that fear.[28] But on account of the strong probability of the opposite opinion, as represented in the positive law theory, it remains doubtful whether such a marriage is valid or invalid. Such being the case, the presumption must stand for the validity of the marriage.[29]

---

25 D. (50, 17) 116; also listed in Reiffenstuel, *De Regulis Juris,* Caput tertium, n. 116.

26 Sangmeister, *Force and Fear,* p. 166; Gasparri, *De Matrimonio,* n. 843; Petrovits, *The New Church Law on Matrimony* (2. ed., Philadelphia: McVey, 1926), n. 427.

27 S. C. S. Off., instr. (ad Ep. Albaniae), 15 febr. 1901—*Fontes,* n. 1250. Cited also by Gasparri, *De Matrimonio,* n. 843.

28 Payen, *De Matrimonio,* II, n. 1690, (1).

29 Cappello, *De Matrimonio,* n. 610; Sangmeister, *Force and Fear,* p. 163; Canon 1014: *in dubio standum est pro valore matrimonii.* See above, p. 46, for a reference to Schmalzgrueber on this point.

The same presumption for validity will hold when the doubt is one of fact, for instance, whether fear in a particular case is grave or slight.[30] If the two infidels in question are subjects of a civil authority that has actually passed a law which makes marriages from force and fear void, the parties are certainly obliged by that law, and cannot give a valid consent if they are under the influence of the invalidating fear.[31]

If one of the infidels should be converted and wish to contract marriage with a baptized person, the privilege of the faith can be invoked in his favor. Whether the civil authority governing him had or lacked a law regarding forced marriages, a positive doubt exists regarding the validity of his first marriage. In his case canon 1014 is overruled by canon 1127: *In re dubia privilegium fidei gaudet favore iuris.* If he is baptized he is entitled to contract the second marriage, with a Catholic party, the usual interpellations having been omitted, even though it is known that the other infidel party of the first marriage is willing to live peacefully with the convert.[32] The more extensive privilege of the faith is here being used[33]rather than the Pauline privilege.[34] Vlaming is of the opinion that the Holy See should be consulted.[35]

SECTION 2. MARRIAGES OF INFIDELS WITH BAPTIZED PARTIES

Not only the natural law, but also the law of the Church applies to a marriage contracted under the influence of fear, between an infidel party and a baptized party, whether the latter is or is not

---

[30] Sangmeister, *Force and Fear,* p. 163.

[31] Sangmeister, *loc. cit.*; Gasparri, *De Matrimonio,* n. 842, and nn. 240-256. In the latter place, Gasparri goes to some length to prove that the civil authority can lay impedient and diriment impediments to the marriages of infidels. His chief argument, which he terms the intrinsic argument, is that the civil authority has to supply for infidels what the Church has given for the baptized, otherwise the author of nature would not have sufficiently provided for civil relationships.—(n. 241). He holds this as certain doctrine.—(n. 240).

[32] Payen, *De Matrimonio,* II, n. 1690; Sangmeister, *loc. cit.*

[33] Canon, 1127.

[34] Canons 1120-1126.

[35] *Praelectiones Iuris Matrimonii ad Normam Codicis Iuris Canonici* (3. ed., 2 vols., Bussum, 1919-1921), II, n. 540 *in fin.* (hereafter cited *Praelectiones*).

a Catholic. In the present discussion it is supposed that a dispensation from the impediment of disparity of cult was obtained by the Catholic, and it is noted that such a dispensation is not needed by a baptized non-Catholic.[36]

If the baptized party was forced into the marriage, the marriage is certainly invalid. The baptized party, Catholic or non-Catholic, comes under the law of the Church in this matter by canon 87. The marriage is invalid because his consent is juridically inefficacious by the law of the Church.[37]

But if the infidel party had contracted under the influence of fear while the baptized party was free, there is some difference of opinion among the authors. Granted that the natural law itself invalidates such marriages, there would be no difficulty in holding the marriage to be invalid, since both classes, baptized and infidels, are bound by the natural law. But proponents of the positive law theory maintain that such a marriage would be valid, at least according to ecclesiastical law. In their opinion the consent as given by the infidel does not come under the law of the Church, and thus is not rendered inefficacious.[38]

The opposite opinion, and by far the more probable one,[39] maintains that the marriage is invalid. The Church, though it cannot directly bind infidels by its laws, can do so indirectly by laying a restriction on the faithful which prevents the latter from contracting marriage in certain circumstances, inasmuch as the Church requires a capacity for marriage in both the parties.[40]

Again, force and fear are set up in the law as hindrances to marriage, not so much in restraint of the agent who inflicts the fear, as for the protection of the liberty of the parties who contract marriage. This liberty is threatened whether the fear be caused by a third party or by the baptized consort. In either case

---

[36] Canon 1070; Payen, *loc. cit.*

[37] Payen, *De Matrimonio,* II, n. 1690; Gasparri, *De Matrimonio,* n. 842; Sangmeister, *Force and Fear,* pp. 163-164.

[38] Gasparri, *De Matrimonio,* n. 842. Juarez (*Vis et Metus,* p. 49), following Gasparri's opinion, denies that there is any foundation at all for the opinion of Wernz-Vidal, Cappello, etc., stating: *Sed vellem scire ubinam existit haec lex inhabilitans Ecclesiae, quam invocant isti auctores.*

[39] Payen, *De Matrimonio,* II, n. 1690.

[40] Wernz-Vidal, *Ius Matrimoniale,* n. 501, note 29.

the law would fall short of its purpose if it did not invalidate this type of marriage. The serious evils which result through a marriage contracted under force and fear are here present in the marriage of a baptized person. The Church could not be true to its mission if it connived at the use of force and fear by a third party through the fact that it still regarded the resulting marriage as valid. Nor could the Church lend countenance to the use of force and fear by a baptized party in that it would honor the marriage in question as a valid union.[41]

Although the opinion which holds that a marriage between an infidel and a baptized party is invalid even if the infidel party has suffered the fear may be considered as by far the more probable opinion, a declaration of nullity could not be given. There is a doubt of law here, and the intervention of the Holy See would be required.[42]

If the parties should desire to regularize the marriage once the element of fear has ceased, then they must renew their matrimonial consent in accordance with the requirements stated in canon 1136.[43]

SECTION 3. MARRIAGES BETWEEN TWO BAPTIZED PARTIES

If the validity of a marriage between two Catholics is questioned on the head of force and fear, the only legal means of settling the issue is a formal trial before a competent ecclesiastical court.[44] Similarly, a marriage between a Catholic and either a baptized non-Catholic or an infidel could be impugned on the head of force and fear only in a formal judicial trial. Because of his baptism,

---

[41] Wernz-Vidal, *Ius Matrimoniale, loc. cit.;* Payen, *De Matrimonio, loc. cit.;* Cappello, *De Matrimonio,* n. 610; Sangmeister, *Force and Fear,* p. 164; Chelodi-Ciprotti, *De Matrimonio,* n. 120; Vromant, *De Matrimonio,* n. 194.

[42] Payen, *De Matrimonio,* II, n. 1690; Vromant, *De Matrimonio,* n. 194.

[43] Vromant, *loc. cit.*

[44] Canons 1960; 1557-1568. The summary process of canon 1990 could not be used even if incontrovertible documentary evidence were at hand. Force and fear cases cannot be adjudicated according to the ruling stated in canon 1990, since this canon does not include mention of the hindrance of force and fear in its all-inclusive listing. Cf. the letter of the Apostolic Delegation at Washington, September 23, 1938 (Bouscaren, *The Canon Law Digest* [2 vols., Milwaukee: The Bruce Publishing Co., Vol. I, 1934, and Vol. II, 1943], II, 531-532). The Pontifical Commission for the Authentic

the Catholic's marriage is subject to the exclusive jurisdiction of the Church.[45]

The problem is somewhat different for a "force and fear" marriage between two baptized non-Catholics. Neither party, as long as he or she remain a non-Catholic, can be a plaintiff in a matrimonial cause,[46] whether before the Tribunal of the Sacred Roman Rota, or before diocesan courts.[47] The diocesan tribunal itself may not institute a trial for exploring the nullity of a marriage between non-Catholics when notice has been given by a Catholic who is living illegitimately with one of the non-Catholic parties. In such circumstances, recourse must be had in each case to the Holy Office.[48]

It is true that apart from any previous permission from the Holy Office the promoter of justice can impugn a marriage when it has been denounced as null by the non-Catholic party of that union, if at the same time in the judgment of the Ordinary the case is of such a nature that the consideration of the public good calls for the intervention of the promoter of justice.[49]

But cases of force and fear are at least normally not to be considered as involving the public good. They fall rather under the category of the private good. There is question here, not of public or occult impediments as referred to in canon 1037, but of an impediment that is or is not of its nature public. By canon 1971, § 1, 2°, the promoter of justice may intervene for the impugning of a marriage solely on the count that the impediment is

---

Interpretation of the Code settled the question beyond all doubt through its reply on December 6, 1943, ad I (*AAS*, XXXVI [1944], 94; Doheny, *Informal Procedure*, pp. 187-188, note 3) which stated that the excepted cases were listed in canon 1990 in all their completeness (*taxative*), and not simply by way of example. The contrary opinion of Cappello (*De Matrimonio*, n. 891, 7) can therefore no longer be upheld.

[45] Canon 87; Cappello, *De Matrimonio*, n. 866.

[46] Cf. the reply of the Holy Office, January 27, 1928—*AAS*, (1928), 75; Bouscaren, *The Canon Law Digest*, II, 762-763.

[47] Cf. the reply of the Holy Office, March 22, 1939, ad I—*AAS*, XXXI (1939), 131; Bouscaren, *The Canon Law Digest*, II, 533-534.

[48] Cf. the private reply of the Holy Office, November 30, 1931—Bouscaren, *The Canon Law Digest*, II, 543.

[49] Cf. the reply of the Holy Office, March 22, 1939, ad II—*AAS*, XXXI (1939), 131; Bouscaren, *The Canon Law Digest*, II, 547.

by its very nature a public impediment. Hence the distinction rests between impediments and hindrances originating in public law (*iuris publici*) or in private law (*iuris privati*). But the nullity of a marriage on the count of force and fear is a matter which depends upon a hindrance established in private law, and not upon a consideration which of its very nature is of public import.[50] Hence the promotor of justice cannot impugn such a marriage on his own initiative, unless by rare exception the public good should actually be involved. Recourse to the Holy See would have to be made for permission to institute the case.

Throughout this discussion on the manner of solving force and fear marriages between two baptized non-Catholics, it has been seen that there is a continual insistence by the Church that the non-Catholic parties do not have the right, but may be granted the privilege, of a *trial* in an ecclesiastical tribunal. Though it is not mentioned specifically, the necessity of holding a formal trial seems to be taken for granted.

De Becker (1857-1936), however, suggested that a "force and fear" marriage between two non-Catholics could be solved along the lines of an investigation into the free status for marriage on the side of the parties. This would do away with the need of employing the formal procedure, which the Church does use for these cases; but De Becker further raised the question "whether the competent Ordinary *must* use the full judicial procedure."[51]

De Becker's argument is summarized in this and the following paragraph. The norms of judicial procedure are intended to have application to a marriage *celebrated* before the Church—consider the wording of canon 1964. Therefore the marriages of baptized non-Catholics do not fall under the general rules of procedure, particularly not when there is question of determining the competent authority for judging the *status liber* (as happens when the parties have moved to a place far distant from the place of contract).

Furthermore there is a practical impossibility of observing the

---

[50] *Decisiones,* XX (1928), 405-407; Bouscaren, *The Canon Law Digest,* II, 544; Wernz-Vidal, *Ius Matrimoniale,* n. 698.

[51] De Becker, *De Matrimonio Praelectiones Canonicae* (ed. nova, Louvain: Ceuterick, 1931), pp. 281-283, Scholion (hereafter cited *De Matrimonio*).

law in such cases, regarding the competent judge, since the judge of the place of contract can hardly obtain suitable documents, since the marriage was not celebrated before the Church. A reply from the Holy Office suggests the shorter procedure: "*Quando vero agitur de matrimonio mixto contrahendo cum haeretico separato per divortii sententiam tribunalis civilis ad haeretica, erit Episcopus domicilii partis catholicae, ad quem spectat iudicare an contrahentes gaudeant status libertate.*"[52] There is a great difference between judicial procedure and the judgment of the Ordinary regarding the *status liber*—confer canon 1020, which states in § 3: "The local Ordinary has the right to prescribe special regulations for this examination of the parties by the pastor."[53]

It seems that the theory of De Becker cannot be accepted for the following reasons. Relative to the regulation of competency as stated in canon 1964, one can say that it is not so much the *fact* as the *locality* in connection with the celebration of a marriage that furnishes the reason for connecting the element of judicial competency with the *locus contractus,* i. e., the search for the truth of the matter has more hope for success if held at the place where the questioned contract was made. This obtains altogether apart from the fact whether the marriage ceremony was or was not performed before the Church. Furthermore, the rest of canon 1964, which in addition connects the element of competency with the factor of domicile or quasi-domicile, does not at all take into consideration the fact of a marriage's *celebration* in a given place, on which factor De Becker so strongly insisted.

Again, even if the investigation into the circumstances of the force and fear were made informally along the lines of an investigation into the *status liber,* it would have to be comparatively lengthy anyway. Witnesses would have to be called, and the possible intricacies underlying the motives of the witnesses and the parties in their testimony and deposition would prohibit a speedy solution. The amount of time consumed would be about the same as for a formal trial. It is true that a second trial would have to be held for the purpose of obtaining the required two concordant judgments declarative of the nullity of the marriage,[54] but the very

---

52 S. C. S. Off. Colonien., 23 iun. 1903—*Fontes,* n. 1266.

53 Translation from Woywod-Smith, *Commentary,* I, 573.

54 Canons 1986-1987.

difficulty of arriving at the full truth (as urged by De Becker) sets up a reasonable demand for the further guarantee that comes only with a formal trial. The replies of the Holy Office, noted above,[55] were given after the promulgation of the Code, and, as was there observed, the necessity of holding a formal trial seemed to be taken for granted. The same can be said of the private reply of the Holy Office, given on April 8, 1925, to the Archbishop of Freiburg: recourse was required before the *tribunal* could act.[56]

Again, the reply of the Holy Office[57] appealed to by De Becker states: "it shall be the bishop . . . to whom it pertains to *judge* whether . . ." in reply to the question that asked which bishop "should institute the *process*." The grounds as presented by De Becker for justifying the dispensing with a formal procedure seem to remain without sufficient warrant. Furthermore, the reply to which he appeals was given before the promulgation of the Code; hence there is at least some doubt whether it can rightly be regarded as still in force. Even if it is, there is still the insistence upon the *process*.

Finally, De Becker refers to the difficulty of obtaining information. This in itself seems rather to call for the formal procedure. Consider the regulation for excepted cases. By canon 1992, if the documentary evidence in a summary procedure is considered unsatisfactory by the tribunal of second instance, the case must be handled by way of a formal trial. In the case discussed here, the documentary evidence is by far the lesser part of the evidence; "force and fear" cases depend for the most part on such evidence as witnesses can supply for establishing the fact that force and fear were inflicted.

---

[55] Cf. *supra*, p. 57.

[56] Cf. Bouscaren, *The Canon Law Digest*, I, 763, note; *Periodica de Re Canonica et Morali* (Brugis, 1905—; ab anno 1927: *Periodica de Re Canonica, Morali, Liturgica*, Brugis (1927-1936) et Romae, 1937—), XIV (1925). 166-167 (hereafter cited *Periodica*).

[57] Cf. *supra*, p. 59.

CHAPTER III

REVERENTIAL FEAR

Reverential fear will invalidate a marriage if it satisfies the conditions stated in canon 1087. This is evident, for such a fear can derive from without, be unjustly inflicted, and inflicted in such a way that the affected party is forced to choose marriage in order to free himself from the fear. Furthermore, this fear can be grave in character. Reverential fear is in and of itself considered as a slight fear, and in the external forum it is presumed to be such. However, it may become grave through the attendant circumstances. The analysis of these attendant circumstances remains a necessary task if one is to gain a full understanding of the nature of reverential fear.

For example, reverential fear need not be attended with threats or cruelty before it can be considered as grave in character. Importunate pleadings or excessively urgent persuasions could make the fear to be grave. An effectively pertinacious will and dominating command on the part of the parent could do the same. These pleadings, requests, and demands are all the more easily considered to be grave if by temperament and character the child is very easily influenced by parental threats and readily victimized by the fear which then sets in.

But caution must be used if one is to make a proper application regarding the notion of reverential fear. A child may contract a marriage at the request of his parents in simple consequence of his customary obedience to them, and in this case the child is not to be regarded as acting with substantial unwillingness.[1] It may well be that the child acts with some reluctance. This is in itself easily understandable even in a person who enters a marriage when motivated through his customary obedience in respect of parental authority.[2]

---

[1] De Lugo, *Disputationes de Iustitia et Iure,* disp. XXII, n. 150.

[2] This summary is adapted from a Rota case. Cf. *Decisiones,* XXVI (1934), 226.

ARTICLE 1. DISTINCTIONS

Reverential fear may be defined as a discerning of a future evil that comes to us from those under whose lawful power we live and in whose regard we sense a duty of homage and respect.[3] Reverential fear usually connotes a fear of the anger of one's parents along with the resultant evils.[4] The basic motive for reverential fear is the reverence for one's superior. Hence it may be considered as a fear that influences an inferior to consent to some contract in deference to his superior; the inferior is in a way coerced and would otherwise be unwilling, but in consequence of his sense of shame and reverence does not dare to contradict the superior for fear of offending him.[5]

Since a classification of types and degrees of reverential fear involves the basic mental attitude of fear, it is difficult and more or less impractical to insist upon a rigid demarcation of types. The following divisions are made, but with the qualification that one type frequently and easily overlaps another. Again, the chief problem in reverential fear is to determine whether it is grave or slight; it is comparatively easy to determine whether reverential fear in a given case is unjust, or inflicted from without, or inflicted in such a manner that the affected party must choose marriage to free himself from the fear.

It has been the consistent jurisprudence of the Rota to consider reverential fear as being in and of itself slight in character. Attendant circumstances may or may not make it grave.[6] There is some disagreement among the authors in defining reverential fear,

---

[3] Pontius, *De Sacramento Matrimonii,* Lib. IV, cap. 5, n. 1—*Decisiones,* XXIX (1937), 86; St. Alphonsus, *Theologia Moralis* (ed. nova, cura et studio P. Leonardi Gaudé, 4 vols., Romae, 1905-1912), Lib. VI, n. 1056.

[4] Ayrinhac, *Marriage Legislation in the New Code of Canon Law* (New York, 1918), n. 206 (hereafter cited *Marriage Legislation*).

[5] Reiffenstuel, Lib. I, tit. 40, n. 94; De Angelis, *Praelectiones Iuris Canonici ad methodum Decretalium Gregorii IX exactae* (5 vols. in 9, Romae, 1877-1891), Lib. I, tit. 40, n. 3 (hereafter cited *Praelectiones*).

[6] *Decisiones,* XIX (1927), 257; *Decisiones,* XXXI (1939), 20, 26; Vermeersch-Creusen, *Epitome,* II, n. 375. In this respect the observation of Hostiensis (d. 1271) with regard to those who are too easily influenced by fear may be added: *Is meticulosus dicitur qui timet timenda et non timenda—In Quinque Decretalium Libros Commentaria* (5 vols. in 3, Venetiis, 1581), Lib. I, tit. 40, c. 4, n. 8.

in view of the different emphasis they place on the subjective or objective elements. However, the difference is not enough to cause difficulty in determining the gravity of the fear.[7]

The basic division of reverential fear is into the two classes, mere reverential fear and qualified reverential fear.[8] Mere reverential fear derives its influence from the reverence or deference which is due to parents or superiors. Since the sense of reverence in an inferior is a perfectly normal factor, it can rarely happen that grave fear would be involved in it. Qualified reverential fear results from the additional circumstances which can make reverential fear grave in character.

Reverential fear is a type of fear. It is amenable to all the conditions noted in canon 1087. But generally the expression reverential fear is considered as the equivalent of mere reverential fear, and hence as slight in character. With the addition of some of the attendant circumstances, in various combinations, the fear becomes a qualified reverential fear, which can easily be grave in character.[9]

The two principal elements in reverential fear are the subjection of the inferior and his consequent fear of the indignation of his superior. Without these two elements the notion of reverential fear could hardly be conceived.[10]

Article 2. Mere Reverential Fear

Even mere reverential fear admits of degrees. The lowest degree is that which involves only the sense of deference and the embarrassment or shame resulting from the refusal to obey. Obviously a real fear could be involved, since there is present an evil that affects the inferior personally. But it is only a slight evil, and can cause only slight fear.[11]

The next higher degree is the fear of causing sadness, displeasure, or offense to one's superior. Strictly considered, a real

---

[7] *Decisiones,* XVIII (1926), 94; Doheny, *Formal Procedure,* p. 897, note 85.

[8] See pp. 5-7, above.

[9] *AAS,* V (1913), 555-556; *Decisiones,* V (1913), 463-464.

[10] *Decisiones,* XXX (1938), 396.

[11] Coronata, *De Matrimonio,* n. 471; Payen, *De Matrimonio,* II, n. 1683.

fear can hardly be said to be present, since the evil is not personal to the inferior. At any rate the fear is normally slight. The highest degree is the fear of the anger of one's parents or superiors. This is a real fear, personal to the inferior, but normally is likewise to be considered as slight. Hence, in general, the three types of mere reverential fear connote the presence of but a slight fear.

Payen suggested that a daughter could be so influenced through filial piety that she would go to great lengths to avoid causing sadness or displeasure in her parents, inasmuch as she would consider these reactions as evils proper to herself, so that as a result her fear, though merely reverential, could be grave. In the light of this, Payen suggested that a marriage thus contracted would be invalid in the internal forum, but in the external forum there would be a lack of sufficient proof for declaring the presence of that effect.[12]

The important problem here relates to the element of indignation in the parents or the superior. Once the anger or indignation becomes protracted and serious, so that it exists as a real threat to the peace of mind of the inferior, the fear becomes grave. The fear becomes modified through these added notes, and thus is usually termed a qualified reverential fear. Circumspect caution is in order when one reads the Rota cases. When using the term "qualified," the recording auditor does not always mean that the fear is necessarily grave; rather, he may simply insinuate that a close analysis usually will establish the actual gravity of the fear. This will be discussed in the following article.

Article 3. Qualified Reverential Fear

Since the various circumstances tend to make the divisions of reverential fear overlap, the more detailed analysis of these circumstances has been reserved to this article.

As was noted above, the term "qualified" with reference to reverential fear must be taken in the sense that this type of fear is usually but not necessarily grave. But many Rota cases use the term "qualified" without making this distinction.[13]

---

[12] *De Matrimonio,* II, n. 1683.

[13] E. g., *Decisiones,* XXVIII (1936), 433, 470, 497, 659, 675, 705, 714; *Decisiones,* XXXI (1939), 131, 194, 405, 479. Coronata (*De Matrimonio,* n. 477) does the same.

The first problem with reference to qualified reverential fear is that of the anger or indignation of the parents or the superiors. If this anger is grave and prolonged it may produce grave fear in the inferior. It is a real and personal evil for the inferior and may easily influence the will of the inferior.[14]

In this, as in the other problems of qualified reverential fear, it is to be noted that the fear can be grave either in its subjective or in its objective elements; it can be relatively grave in consequence of the personalities and relationships involved. This is especially true in reverential fear.[15]

But another element must be considered together with this. It is the problem of the ingrained obedience which children show toward their parents and by which they submit to their parents' behests, even though occasionally they experience some diffidence or even repugnance. Rota cases and authors usually refer to this with the phrase *"morem ut gerat."*[16] If children act through customary obedience, then they do not perform their acts under the coercion of reverential fear, unless at the same time they are really unwilling.[17]

Usually the meaning attached to the idea of the customary obedience (*morem gerere*) which does not imply any invalidating element for the marriage is to be understood of a child who, knowing the wish of his parents, accedes to their wish immediately or

---

[14] Coronata, *De Matrimonio,* n. 471; *AAS,* III (1911), 663—*Decisiones,* III (1911), 334; *Decisiones,* XXI (1929), 105; Pontius, *De Sacramento Matrimonii,* Lib. IV, cap. 5, n. 7; Payen, *De Matrimonio,* II, n. 1683; Sanchez, *De Matrimonii Sacramento,* Lib. IV, disp. VI, n. 7; Gasparri, *De Matrimonio,* n. 848; Ojetti, *Synopsis Rerum Moralium et Iuris Pontificii alphabetico ordine digesta* (3. ed., 4 vols., Romae, 1909-1914), s. v. *Metus,* n. 2740 (hereafter cited *Synopsis*).

[15] *Decisiones,* XVI (1924), 139; *Decisiones,* XXXI (1939), 26; Blat, *Commentarium Textus Iuris Canonici* (5 vols. in 6, Vol. III [*De Rebus*], Pars I [*De Sacramentis*], 2. ed., Romae, 1924), *De Sacramentis,* p. 610 (hereafter cited *De Sacramentis*).

[16] Sanchez, *De Matrimonii Sacramento,* Lib. IV, disp. IX, n. 12: *ut morem illis gerat, quos reveretur et amat, et quibus ob multa alia indiget."* Cf. *Decisiones,* XXX (1938), 223-224.

[17] Gasparri, *De Matrimonio,* n. 848; De Lugo, *Disputationes de Iustitia et Iure,* disp. XXII, nn. 145-146, 150; *Decisiones,* XXIX (1937), 603, 783; *Decisiones,* XXVIII (1936), 183; *Decisiones,* XXX (1938), 69, 224; *Decisiones,* XXXI (1939), 27.

with only some brief hesitation.[18] If the child is absolutely unwilling and yet obeys through fear, one can no longer say that he acts exclusively through customary obedience; obviously he is not acting through habit alone, nor is he acting according to his own will.[19]

Reverential fear can also become grave when it is qualified by importunities, pleas, entreaties and the like, when these have become so ceaseless and insistent that they overcome the resistance of the affected party.[20] These pleas, etc., must be often repeated, sufficiently frequent, and importunate enough to establish grave fear. An occasional plea, or a strong entreaty as an isolated fact, would not establish the constant pressure on the will that would be needed to build up the grave fear.[21]

Again, the gravity will depend upon the sensibilities and susceptibilities of the persons involved, since it is in the presence of these that the fear may become at least relatively grave. The insistence of the pleas must constitute a real coercion in the mind of the inferior, so that he becomes convinced that he no longer has at his disposal any means for an effective resistance.[22] This coercion can be established especially when the superior is determined at all costs to attain his end.[23] The Rota has consistently held that such pleas and importunities can constitute a qualified or grave fear.[24]

The problem is somewhat different with reference to a command given by the parent or the superior. Since a command has

---

[18] *Decisiones*, XXIX (1937), 603.

[19] *Decisiones*, XXVIII (1936), 558; *Decisiones*, XXXI (1939), 131.

[20] Doheny, *Formal Procedure*, p. 897; Reiffenstuel, Lib. I, tit. 40, n. 95.

[21] Schmalzgrueber, Lib. IV, tit. 1, n. 5; Ojetti, *Synopsis*, s. v. *Metus*, n. 2740; Sanchez, *De Matrimonii Sacramento*, Lib. IV, disp. VII, nn. 7-8; *Decisiones*, XIV (1922), 4; *Decisiones*, XXIX (1937), 41; *Decisiones*, XXXI (1939), 459.

[22] Cosci, *De Separatione Tori Coniugalis* (folio ed., 3 Libri in 2 vols., Romae, 1773-1779—and later ed., Lib. I and II only, in 1 vol., Florentiae, 1856), Lib. I, cap. VIII, nn. 73-74, and Lib. I, cap. XVI, nn. 221-222.

[23] Pignatelli, *Consultationes Canonicae* (9 vols. in 5, Coloniae Allobrogum, 1700, and supplement, Cosmopoli, 1711), Tom. IX, Consult. 180, n. 19; *Decisiones*, XIV (1922), 5; *Decisiones*, XVI (1924), 327.

[24] *Decisiones*, XVI (1924), 164; *Decisiones*, XXI (1929), 105-106; *Decisiones*, XIX (1927), 406; *Decisiones*, XXXI (1939), 479.

more moral force than a request or plea, the command need not be repeated as often as the plea in order to have the same effect. In consequence of the nature of a command it can be seen that a single and unrepeated command could be equal to or stronger than a series of repeated pleas. Ciprotti brings this out in a discussion of the recent Rota jurisprudence.[25]

According to canon 1087 the fear must derive from without before it can invalidate a marriage. Hence, for the parent to exert pressure that would result in reverential fear, he would have to do so by means of some external act.[26] He can do this by means of an explicit command. Authors have not dealt much with the question of parental commands which induce a qualified reverential fear. But in the present century the Rota has discussed it in various decisions.[27]

It seems that an imperious command[28] can establish a grave fear. The mere reverential fear already present becomes qualified through the virtual threat. If the command is imperious and stated with severity, it amounts to a demand which suggests very strongly that unpleasant consequences will follow upon a refusal. Even though the command is not repeated, the child will fear the ensuing anger, which he is sure will come if he knows his parents are usually determined to carry out their plans at all costs. The explicit threat is not needed.[29]

If the parents or the superiors are of a pertinacious will, strongly and effectively insistent that they be obeyed without question, an imperious command given by them will have more effect than repeated pleas or importunities.[30] Massimi, as Dean of the Roman

---

25 "Iurisprudentia S. R. Rotae de metu reverentiali ex parentum iussu," *Apollinaris,* XIV (1941), 84-88 (hereafter cited "De metu ex parentum iussu"); cf. also Chelodi-Ciprotti, *De Matrimonio,* n. 119, *bis.*

26 *Decisiones,* XXIII (1931), 415.

27 Ciprotti, "De metu ex parentum iussu" n. 2, *Apollinaris,* XIV (1941), 85-86; *Decisiones,* XX (1928), 273, 283; *Decisiones,* XXI (1929), 314; *Decisiones,* XXIII (1931), 12.

28 Cf. *Decisiones,* XXIII (1931), 12, where the expression *"austera iussio"* is used.

29 Ciprotti, "De metu ex parentum iussu" n. 3, *Apollinaris,* XIV (1941), 87; Cosci, *De Separatione Tori Coniugalis,* Lib. III, cap. IV, n. 80.

30 Ciprotti, "De metu ex parentum iussu," n. 3, *Apollinaris,* XIV (1941), 86.

Rota, continued maintaining the doctrine he had presented in the Rota decisions quoted above[31] by repeating it in further decisions seven years later.[32]

Many modern authors do not treat the problem specifically, and usually refer only to the imperious character of the parent as being capable of causing grave fear in connection with importunities and explicit or virtual threats.[33] Coronata states that the command of an imperious father is generally considered a cause of grave and unjust fear for the reason that it contains implicit threats.[34]

Threats, whether explicit or implicit, can be present with any or all of the circumstances of qualified reverential fear noted above. There is little difficulty in admitting that explicit threats can constitute grave fear.[35] Granted that a grave evil has been threatened, and that there is moral certainty that the threat can and will be carried out if the inferior does not comply with the wishes of the superior, then a grave qualified reverential fear is established. If a grave evil is threatened by one who is accustomed to carry out his threats, the resultant fear in the threatened party is grave.[36]

But implicit or virtual threats can also bring about grave fear. As long as the affected party is convinced that his parents are surely going to afflict him with some grave evil, the presence of grave fear is established. It make no difference whether the threat of evil was explicit or implicit or virtual. The party has been unjustly and wrongfully treated by his parents.[37]

---

[31] *Decisiones,* XX (1928), 273, 283.

[32] *Decisiones,* XXVII (1935), 275, 403. Page 403 gives the following: *Ita, ad metum reverentialem qualificandum, satis est pertinacis violentisque patris imperium vel aequivalens agendi ratio, cui filius se subtrahere non valeat, quamvis protestetur se nolle eas nuptias inire.* Cf. also a recent case *Decisiones,* XXXI (1939), 562.

[33] Blat, *De Sacramentis,* p. 610; Sangmeister, *Force and Fear,* p. 147; Doheny, *Formal Procedure,* p. 897—in note 85 here, Doheny quotes a Rota case (*Decisiones,* XX (1928), 364), in which it was stated: *Patris imperium satis esse potest, ut metus reverentialis habeatur pro gravi, si filius etc.;* Payen, *De Matrimonio,* II, n. 1683; Gasparri, *De Matrimonio,* n. 848.

[34] *De Matrimonio,* n. 471, *in fine.*

[35] *Decisiones,* XXXI (1939), 19, 522-523.

[36] *Decisiones,* XIV (1922), 297-298; Cosci, *De Separatione Tori Coniugalis,* Lib. I, cap. VIII, n. 79; Coronata, *De Matrimonio,* n. 471; *Decisiones,* XXIX (1937), 25.

[37] Cf. Hostiensis: *vel alius male tractabatur*—Lib. IV, tit. 1, c. 28, n. 3.

The implicit or virtual threat can cause grave fear, since it can qualify the reverential fear to such an extent that the affected party suffers the loss of his liberty of choice, just as much as if the threat were explicitly made. Previously there had been a difference of opinion on this point.[38] But it is generally admitted that implicit or virtual threats can establish qualified reverential fear, since, as Sanchez observed, "they are virtually present, even though not actually."[39] Recent Rota decisions do not often refer to this specific problem.[40]

An important point to be considered in reference to threats is that threats can more easily establish grave fear if they are made against one who is already influenced by mere reverential fear. Threats not absolutely grave in themselves could increase the fear so that it became a fully qualified reverential fear, sufficiently grave to invalidate the marriage.[41]

But if the threat is absolutely grave, then a common fear is present. Sometimes Rota cases refer to such a fear as reverential fear mixed with common fear, or with fear simply grave. If such fear occurs, the gravity of the fear is more easily proved.[42] Cases of reverential fear mixed with common fear occur frequently, and references to this combination can be found in many volumes of the Rota decisions.[43]

What has been said of threats can be equally applied to blows and other kinds of physical ill-treatment. Blows and ill-treatment can qualify reverential fear and make it grave, even though they may not be absolutely serious in themselves. If they are grave in themselves, the fear is reverential fear mixed with com-

---

38 Sangmeister, *Force and Fear,* p. 147; Rossi, "De consensu matrimoniali," *Analecta Ecclesiastica* (Romae, 1893-1911), XIX (1911), 68.

39 Sangmeister, *Force and Fear,* p. 147; Sanchez, *De Matrimonii Sacramento,* Lib. IV, disp. VI, nn. 12, 14; Cosci, *De Separatione Tori Coniugalis,* Lib. III, cap. IV, n. 77.

40 By exception, there are several explicit references in the 1934 volume: *Decisiones,* XXVI (1934), 49-50, 174, 765, 782.

41 *Decisiones,* XXVIII (1936), 88; *Decisiones,* XXIX (1937), 215.

42 *Decisiones,* XVIII (1926), 152, 157; *Decisiones,* XXIX (1937), 87, 505.

43 *Decisiones,* XIII (1921), 252; *Decisiones,* XVIII (1926), 152; *Decisiones,* XXVII (1935), 318; *Decisiones,* XXVIII (1936), 470; *Decisiones,* XXX (1938), 107, 382-383; *Decisiones,* XXXI (1939), 150.

mon fear, and the gravity of the fear is all the more easily established.[44]

In all these relations between parent and child it is the instilled fear which affects the validity of the marriage, and not the good or bad faith of the parents. The parents may be in good faith the while they unjustly inflict a grave fear. It is the objective injustice, independently of the conscience of the parents, that interferes with the freedom of choice that the child must have.[45] Even a daughter who has attained her majority may be subject to the influence of a qualified reverential fear. The duty of the father is to counsel, to advise, and, according to circumstances, to rebuke in moderation. If he abuses his authority to a sufficient extent, the marriage involved will be invalid.[46]

A marriage will be invalid even if the invalidating fear should be combined with an intrinsic fear. If a daughter were unjustly forced into marriage, even though she be concerned about the needs of her parents, and has some hope of relieving these needs by means of the marriage, the marriage is invalid for, although she has contracted the marriage *with* intrinsic fear, she has also contracted the marriage *through* fear which came from without and was unjustly inflicted.[47]

---

[44] *Decisiones,* XXXI (1939), 150.

[45] *AAS,* IX (1917), 508—*Decisiones,* IX (1917), 29; *Decisiones,* XXXI (1939), 26.

[46] *Decisiones,* XXXI (1939), 131.

[47] *Decisiones,* XXX (1938), 522-523.

CHAPTER IV

APPLICATION TO THE FAR EAST

In this chapter the norms for reverential fear as discussed in the previous chapter will be applied to reverential fear as it occurs in the Far East. No attempt will be made to present the entire sociological background. Only those customs which can directly influence matrimonial consent through reverential fear, or have a sufficiently close connection with that problem, will be included. The chief sources of material will be Rota cases originating in the Far East, and the writings of some non-Catholic authors.

It is hoped that the references to the non-Catholic authors will properly indicate the influence of the pagan customs upon the Chinese Catholics. Some of these customs are inimical, others are or can be neutral, in relation to the Catholic concept of liberty of consent in marriage. The Rota cases here cited should serve to indicate how freedom to marry was interfered with in actual cases in China, and specifically in what measure the long-established customs in China were responsible for this interference. Various Rota cases originating from China, Indo-China, Korea, and Manchuria indicate that the problems of reverential fear arise from customs that are fundamentally similar in this matter. In this chapter, then, discussions of customs in China will be considered as applicable to the other countries, unless an exception is specifically made.

Furthermore, an inquiry will be made into the invalidating force of these customs when they run counter to the prescriptions of canon 1087 on force and fear in marriage. These problems of the parent-child relationship will be taken up in four articles: power of the parents, filial piety of the children, engaged parties, summary.

Article 1. Power of the Parents

Section 1. Nature of the Parental Power

The power of the parents, and especially of the father, over the children is established beyond question, as will be seen from various sources. Due to western influences, there is some mitigation of this power in cities and areas more open to that influence.[1]

The arrangements for the marriage usually are entirely in the hands of the parents. This is true also for Catholic marriages, as is evidenced by cases from Indo-China (Tonkin),[2] from China proper,[3] and Manchuria.[4] This is based on the practically universal custom in pagan China that has obtained through centuries.[5]

The family system resembles the Roman Law family system in many respects. Writers on the family system of China often use the Roman Law terms, such as *patria potestas, manumissio,* etc.[6]

The abuses possible under this system have not been completely uprooted from among the Chinese Catholics. To make the entire negotiation of the marriage depend on the parents *alone* is to inflict an injury upon the children. Parents do not have such a right to impose marriage, nor do the children have a corresponding obligation. A serious presumption of coercion immediately arises, since it seems quite likely that the parents may press their children, however unwilling, into contracting marriage.[7]

The custom is to arrange the marriage for the children. The danger is that the son or the daughter is often not consulted.[8]

---

[1] Cf. p. 20, above.

[2] *AAS,* III (1911), 663; *Decisiones,* III (1911), 334; also *Decisiones,* XVI (1924), 139, 165.

[3] From Luanfu: *Decisiones,* XVIII (1926), 158; from Ning-po: *Decisiones,* XIX (1927), 404.

[4] *AAS,* IX (1917), 505; *Decisiones,* IX (1917), 26.

[5] Werner, *A History of Chinese Civilization* (? vols. Vol. I, Shanghai: The Shanghai Times, 1940, I, 369 (hereafter cited *History*); Werner, *Descriptive Sociology: Chinese* (London, 1910), p. 27, col. 3, *in fin.* (hereafter cited *Sociology*). Werner here quotes the "*China Review* (Hongkong), vi, 64." It is to be noted that Werner's *Sociology* is a compilation of quotations from many books and articles, arranged in logico-chronological form. Cf. again, Werner, *Sociology,* p. 29, col. 1, *in med.,* quoting: "De Groot, *The Religious System of China* (Vols. 1-6 [in progress], Leyden, 1892-1910), ii. i. 615"; Douglas, *Society in China* (London, 1894), pp. 192-193; Shiao-Tung Fei, *Peasant Life in China* (New York: Dutton and Co., 1939), pp. 40-41.

[6] Werner, *History,* I, 367; Werner, *Sociology,* p. 27, col. 3, *in fin.,* quoting: "*China Review,* vi. 64"; Douglas, *Society in China,* p. 110.

[7] *Decisiones,* XVI (1924), 139, 165.

[8] *AAS,* IX (1917), 505; *Decisiones,* IX (1917), 26.

Frequently enough the child does not become informed of the engagement to marry until after all the details are completed, and even up to two days before the marriage.[9] Many inconveniences arise from trying to break that contract, and the temptation will be strong for the parents to force their children into the marriage. The parents' power is strong and assured; among the pagans it can sometimes amount to the power over life and death.[10]

Not only the parents, but also those who stand *in loco parentis* enjoy the same or almost equal power. The power over life and death has been weakened by the recent Civil Code of the Republic of China, and cannot be countenanced by the Catholic Church. But the *patria potestas* will remain in some form. With the death of the father his power passes to the mother, and after her death to the eldest son. There are some exceptions, but usually there is someone with the power to arrange a marriage for a given party.[11] There is even a danger that this power, devolving as it does upon the directors of Catholic orphanages, will be misused, even to the extent of the use of absolute physical force.[12]

Obviously, parents who are conscious of this power may easily be led to grave anger if a child refuses to agree to the marriage.[13] The father would be quick to assert his authority.[14] It is easy to see that the misuse of parental authority can lead to grave fear that would invalidate the marriage. Payen pointed out that Catholic parents in China not infrequently could be wrong in this matter, even though they were in good faith.[15]

---

[9] *AAS,* IX (1917), 505; *Decisiones,* IX (1917), 26.

[10] Werner, *Sociology,* p. 27, col. 2, *in med.,* quoting: "Dudgeon, *Diet, Dress and Dwellings of the Chinese in Relation to Health* (2 vols., London, 1866), pp. 282-283"; Douglas, *Society in China,* p. 110.

[11] Werner, *Sociology,* p. 36, col. 2, *circa fin.,* quoting: *"Journal of the North China Branch of the Royal Asiatic Society, New Series,* (Shanghai), xxvii, 187-188," and referring to "De Groot, *The Religious System of China,* ii. i. 616."

[12] *Decisiones,* XXII (1930), 653.

[13] *Decisiones,* XXI (1929), 109; *Decisiones,* XIX (1927), 404.

[14] *Decisiones,* XIX (1927), 404, 409: *"Il suffit qu'une femme soit du sexe féminin. Regarde autour de toi. Qui a choisi sa femme lui-meme."* . . . *Quamvis puella laboraret foetida infirmitate; Decisiones,* XIV (1922), 297.

[15] *De Matrimonio,* II, n. 1702, (1), *Secundo.*

One reason for this power of the parents, and especially of the father, is the strong desire to perpetuate the family name. Though the roots of this desire may be traced to the pagan custom of ancestor-worship, the legitimate desire of perpetuating the name remains among the Catholics. It can easily be seen that this circumstance may lead the parents to use unjustified duress to bring about a marriage over the protest of an unwilling child. This pressure is all the more easily brought to bear in view of the fact that the individual family is part of the strongly patriarchal system in China. The father would go to great lengths to protect his reputation in the clan for having obedient children and descendants through them.[16]

The civil law of China has not done much to change this customary power of the parents. In the present Code for China, Article 972 insists on the consent of the parties to an engagement to marry; Article 973 sets the minimum age at 17 for the boy and 15 for the girl, for the engagement.[17] This compares closely with the analogous Articles on marriage, as quoted above, where it was observed that the regulations of this Code are very much ignored.[18]

SECTION 2. SPECIFIC USES OF THE PARENTAL POWER

A. *Marriage Engagements*

Both the engagement and the marriage have been and are arranged by the parents, frequently without any consultation of the wishes of the children.[19] The recent Republican legislation as found in the Civil Code has had little effect in changing this custom.[20] The Church has made provision for the formal engage-

---

16 *Decisiones,* XXI (1929), 109; Werner, *History,* I, 332, 369, 391, 397; Werner, *Sociology,* p. 30, col. 1, *post princip.,* quoting: "Möllendorff, *The Family Law of the Chinese* (Shanghai, 1896), p. 28"; Werner, *Sociology,* p. 27, col. 2, *in med.,* quoting: "Dudgeon, *Diet Dress and Dwellings of the Chinese in Relation to Health,* pp. 282-283"; Douglas, *Society in China,* p. 110.

17 Cf. *The Civil Code of the Republic of China.* Cf. also, *Praxis Missionalis in Vicariatu Apostolico de Ichang* (Wuchang: The Franciscan Press, 1935), n. 399 (hereafter cited *Praxis Missionalis*).

18 Cf. p. 20, above; cf. Werner, *History,* I, 332.

19 *Decisiones,* XXII (1930), 653; *History,* I, 332.

20 Werner, *History,* I, 332; *The Civil Code of the Republic of China,* Articles 972-973.

ments entered into with ecclesiastical formalities,[21] and has explicitly done the same for China.[22] Formal engagements in accordance with the requirements enacted in canon 1017 are sometimes made in China,[23] but the real problem is the civil contract of engagement, its financial implications, and the customs connected with it.

There are some abuses connected with the custom of arranging marriages for children without consulting them. These abuses call for some consideration here. Engagements are sometimes arranged for the children before the age of puberty.[24] This is sometimes done for children between the ages of seven and fourteen.[25] The custom has been reprobated by the Church, but it still constitutes a problem.[26] Sometimes the engagement is made for children in infancy.[27] and in comparatively rare cases there have been instances of pre-natal engagements, conditioned only on the circumstance that the children are of different sexes.[28]

Obviously, such arrangements were made for children who for the most part were not old enough to give an ecclesiastically juridical consent to the engagement at the time it was made. As a consequence there was a strong temptation for the parents to coerce the children into ratifying the engagement, and subsequently into giving consent for the marriage. Perhaps the most pernicious

---

21 Canon 1017.

22 *Council of Shanghai,* n. 381, 2°-5°.

23 The writer has had personal experience in this matter.

24 During the Middle Ages the abuse in Europe called for the distinct title *De desponsatione impuberum* in the Decretals; C. 1-14, X, *de desponsatione impuberum,* IV, 2; C. un., *de desponsatione impuberum,* IV, 2, in VI°.

25 *Decisiones,* XXI (1929), 104; *Decisiones,* XIX (1927), 404-405; Werner, *Sociology,* p. 29, col. 1, *post incip.,* quoting: "Gray, *China: A History of the Laws, Manners, and Customs of the People* (2 vols., London, 1878), i. 189" (hereafter cited *China*).

26 *Council of Shanghai,* n. 381, 1°; *Praxis Missionalis,* n. 163, 8°.

27 *Council of Shanghai, loc. cit.; Praxis Missionalis, loc. cit.;* Werner, *History,* I, 313; Werner, *Sociology,* p. 29, col. 1, *post incip.,* quoting: "Gray, *China,* i. 189."

28 Werner, *Sociology,* p. 29, col. 2, *in med.,* quoting: Doolittle, *Social Life of the Chinese* (2 vols., London, 1866), i. 98-99"; Werner, *History,* I, 313. Though rare in occurrence, this practice goes back for centuries. Cf. Werner, *History,* I, 344.

part of the procedure was that the children were often not consulted at all. The Church has never countenanced this practice.[29]

When parents or those who are *in loco parentis* make such arrangements without consulting the child, and if furthermore they pay no attention to the denial of ratification by the child, it is clear that the defenseless child (especially if a girl) can free herself from the pressure brought to bear only by consenting eventually to the marriage. The fear inflicted in such circumstances will easily be grave, and is of course unjust; invalidity of the marriage can easily be involved.[30]

All parents, of course, have the right and duty to supervise their children's marriage engagements. In this matter they may use advice, moderate rebukes, persuasions and requests. This is quite different from serious importunities and vexations, and especially from threats of unjust treatment which are grave in character.[31] The danger is that parents in China are tempted to go beyond reasonable persuasion when they reflect on, if not almost instinctively act on, their rather autocratic powers, which are so customarily taken for granted.

B. *Dowry*

The dowry can also give occasion to the use of force and fear in coercing unwilling children into marriage. The dowry is a settlement of money or property made over by the parents of the prospective groom to the parents of the intended bride. The parents of the girl do not profit much by this arrangement, since a good part of the dowry must be expended on the bride's trousseau.[32]

Once the money and goods (e. g., costly cloths) have been utilized for the tailoring of the wedding clothes and the finery of the bride, the parents would be put to serious financial disadvan-

---

[29] Synod of the Vicariate of Szechuan (*Sutchuensis*) held in 1803: *Collectio Lacensis,* VI, 621—cf. above, pp. 12-14; *Council of Shanghai,* n. 381, 1°-2°; *Praxis Missionalis,* n. 163, 8°; *Decisiones,* XXII (1930), 653; *Decisiones,* XVIII (1926), 158.

[30] *Decisiones,* XXII (1930), 661; *Decisiones,* XVI (1924), 139.

[31] *Decisiones,* XXIX (1937), 783.

[32] *Decisiones,* XIV (1922), 293; *Decisiones,* XVI (1924), 69.

tage in attempting to repay the dowry.[33] This would hold true especially if the parents were poor and probably had already committed themselves to a wedding festivity that taxed their resources, or even put them in debt. If the daughter unreasonably made her objections at this stage, though she had ample opportunity for objecting long before, the parents would be justified in using a fair amount of persuasion and rebuke in order to urge the girl to consent to the marriage. The girl would have to have an adequate reason and explanation to justify her sudden and (presumably) unjustified change of mind.[34]

But if the parents made the engagement without consulting her, and without even asking her ratification, it could happen that the girl was able to summon enough courage to object only when confronted with the imminence of the unwanted marriage. In these circumstances the parents would already have acted unjustly in arranging the engagement without obtaining the girl's consent at any time;[35] now that the dowry had been accepted and expended on the trousseau, the parents would be strongly tempted to use the further unjust means which were discussed above in the chapter on reverential fear.

Even the terminology and the underlying concept in reference to engagement and marriage, as these have been carried over from the pagan customs, can open the way to abuses. The process of arranging for a marriage is often referred to as "buying a wife."[36] Obviously this concept, if accepted with sheer literalness by the parents, could easily lend occasion for the infliction of force and fear on the children, and especially on the daughter.

C. *The "Little Bride"*

It sometime happens that a girl, when her engagement has been arranged by her parents, will be sent to the home of her future

---

[33] *Decisiones,* XIV (1922), 297; *Decisiones,* XIX (1927), 407.

[34] *Council of Shanghai,* n. 381, 5°.

[35] *Council of Shanghai,* n. 381, 1°-2°; *Praxis Missionalis,* n. 163, 8°.

[36] *AAS,* XIII (1921), 54; *Decisiones,* XI (1919), 171; also *Decisiones,* XV (1923), 127; *Decisiones,* XVIII (1926), 220; Werner, *Sociology,* p. 29, col. 3,—p. 30, col. 1, quoting: "Möllendorff, *The Family Law of the Chinese,* pp. 26-28", observing: "By accepting the purchase money, the father of the bride sells and manumits his daughter to the bridegroom's family, to which she henceforth belongs."

husband, where she will take up residence permanently. There will eventually be a wedding ceremony, but in this case usually without much pomp or festivity in the wedding celebration. The reasons for this arrangement may be varied, but a frequent reason is the poverty of the girl's parents, who feel unable or unwilling to rear her. The girl may thus be given away or sold or formally engaged to be the future wife of a son in the family of a friend or a relative. The age of the girl at the time of this arrangement may be that of a few years, or possibly of a few months or weeks. When this arrangement has been made for the girl, she is known as a "little bride."[37]

This arrangement is a much less frequent variation of the usual procedure for marriage engagements.[38] However, it still occurs often enough to draw explicit reprobation from the Church.[39] The dangers arising from the prolonged familiarity of the engaged couple hardly need comment. But the matter here at issue is the danger of an unhappy and even disastrous marriage. The pastor or missionary can permit the "little bride" arrangement only under special conditions and with special safeguards.[40] At a reasonable time before the actual marriage the missionary must take special precautions to assure himself of the full freedom of the girl for giving consent, and unless he is morally certain of the consent of the girl, he must consult the Ordinary.[41]

The "little bride" element has appeared in cases tried before the Rota.[42] This custom could easily give rise to many "force and fear" cases. If one or both of the engaged couple should refuse to contract the expected marriage, the parents would be thoroughly

---

[37] This English term is a literal translation of the Chinese term *hsiao hsi fu* (Mandarin dialect: Wade Romanization). The term is well known to missionaries in China.

[38] Werner, *Sociology,* p. 28, col. 1, *in med.,* quoting: "Doolittle, *Social Life of the Chinese,* i. 98."

[39] *Council of Shanghai,* n. 382, 1°-2°; *Praxis Missionalis,* n. 163, 9°; Payen, *De Matrimonio,* I, n. 341; cf. Winslow, *A Commentary on the Apostolic Faculties* (New York: Field Afar Press, 1946), p. 89.

[40] *Council of Shanghai,* n. 382, 2°; Payen, *De Matrimonio,* I, n. 342.

[41] *Council of Shanghai,* n. 382, 3°.

[42] *Decisiones,* XVIII (1926), 152-153; *Decisiones,* XIX (1927), 409—the sentence of this cause was confirmed in a second trial: *Decisiones,* XXI (1929), 104, where the "little bride" circumstance was again referred to.

angry with them, and the party who showed unwillingness could reasonably expect harsh treatment; grave fear would be an almost certain consequence.[43]

SECTION 3. ATTENDANT CIRCUMSTANCES

A typical note in marriage arrangements is the use of the "middle-man," also known as the "go-between" or "match-maker."[44] It has occurred that the match-maker gives a false report to the two families who are negotiating for the mariage, and the bride and groom may be misinformed about each other up to the very wedding ceremony.[45] If either party should suddenly though reasonably make strong objections to the other party, and refuse to go through with the marriage, even though everything had been arranged, there would be a grave danger of the infliction of force and fear. The infliction would probably be unjust, inasmuch as the party was not informed of facts he was entitled to know, so that he could have indicated his objections at an earlier and more reasonable time.

In this section on attendant circumstances, the questions of threats, ostracism, and physical force need some consideration.

Threats can cause grave fear in the threatened party. According to the conclusions of the previous chapter, even virtual threats can cause grave fear.[46] In view of the great power that parents in China enjoy, it is not surprising that threats of grave evil made by them against their children who refuse to consent to a marriage that has been arranged for them are considered as causing grave fear.[47]

---

[43] Payen, *De Matrimonio,* I, n. 431.

[44] Werner, *Sociology,* p. 29, col. 2, *in princip.,* quoting: "Möllendorff, *The Family Law of the Chinese,* pp. 23-24," and "Williams, *The Middle Kingdom* (2. ed., 2 vols., New York, 1883), i. 786-787" and "Gray, *China,* i. 190-191."

[45] In a Rota case originating from *Ce-li, Meridio-occidentalis* (Manchuria), the bridegroom was deceived until after the wedding ceremony—*AAS,* V (1913), 372-373; *Decisiones,* V (1913), 242-243. However, a declaration of nullity was given on the count of substantial error by way of mistaken identity of person.

[46] Cf. pp. 68-69, above.

[47] *AAS,* V (1913), 553; *Decisiones,* V (1913), 461; also *Decisiones,* XIV (1922), 291, 297-298; *Decisiones,* XVI (1924), 69, 71; *Decisiones,* XVI (1924), 140, 165-166.

This is particularly true in China, since the children have little if any chance of escaping the control of their parents. It is not likely that the children can enlist sympathy and help from others if the parents are determined to force the marriage through at all costs.[48] In fact, if the threat of grave evil is understood by the child as being undoubtedly effective, there is question not only of qualified reverential fear, but also of common fear.[49]

A special type of threat, that of ostracism, can be peculiarly effective in China. From what has been said above concerning parental power and the patriarchal nature of the clan, a child threatened with ostracism is placed at a disastrous disadvantage. In the first place, the child would be considered, rightly or wrongly, as having brought shame and disgrace to his parents,[50] and thus might find life next to impossible in the locality inhabited by his clan. On the other hand, the child would know that he faced a bleak prospect if he left that locality entirely. Other clans would not be inclined to receive him, since they would consider his departure from his clan as an automatic mark of suspicion against him. Refuge in the anonymity of the large cities would also mean hardship for the child, even if he were strong-willed and self-reliant.

The threat of ostracism in China is not unheard of,[51] and if effectively made can cause qualified reverential fear, or even simply grave (or common) fear.[52]

With regard to blows much the same thing can be said. An angered parent, conscious of his power, could readily feel inclined to beat the reluctant child, and thus the consequent fear could well be a common fear rather than only a qualified reverential fear.[53]

---

[48] Cf. a case of the Rota, not from the Far East—*Decisiones,* XX (1928), 364.

[49] *Decisiones,* XXVI (1934), 564.

[50] *Decisiones,* XIX (1927), 409.

[51] *Decisiones,* XVI (1924), 68-69.

[52] *Decisiones,* XVIII (1926), 152.

[53] *Decisiones,* XVIII (1926), 152-157; *AAS,* V (1913), 256-257—*Decisiones,* V (1913), 55-57. Cf. p. 22, above.

Article 2. Filial Piety of the Children

The great power of the parents over their children presupposes an accustomed if not automatic obedience in the children. The notion of filial piety is taught to the children incessantly by word, example and circumstances. To some extent this militates against the development of independent ideas and action on the part of the children, even when they approach maturity.[54] The Rota has made a pertinent observation on this point:

> If among the Chinese it is the custom for the children to follow the will of their parents in entering marriage, this can be tolerated only in so far as the children do not manifest a contrary will, in which case that custom is to be reprobated as unjust.[55]

Added to this is the fact that the child will sense a repugnance, clearly a strong form of reverential fear, toward being considered an unfilial child, thus bringing disgrace on the family. The force of this repugnance is indicated in a later Rota case.[56]

But from accustomed obedience the child will be inclined to obey his parents in the matter of marriage. Even though the child may feel a comparatively strong distaste for his intended spouse, he may not voice his objections at all, or may make a weak representation of his views.[57] Being then commanded by his parents to go through with the arrangement he will acquiesce (for this case it is supposed that the parents do not use overbearing pressure or grave harshness). In such a case there is no more than mere reverential fear. The marriage would be valid, since the consent had been influenced only by means of a mere reverential, that is, a slight fear. Admittedly, the child was in a difficult situation, and decided to take marriage as the only way out. But a

---

54 Werner, *History,* I, 399, quoting: "Lin Yutang, *My Country and My People* (2. ed., New York: John Day with Reynal and Hitchcock, 1938), pp. 176-177."

55 *AAS,* IX (1917), 508; *Decisiones,* IX (1917), 29; also *Decisiones,* XVIII (1926), 158.

56 *Decisiones,* XXI (1929), 109—the text is italicized as follows: " . . . j'aurais *été considéré comme un mauvais fils* si j'avais osé desobéir."

57 By custom, the girl is also expected from a sense of modesty to refrain from discussing her engagement, and even to delay her assent to the engagement when informed of it.—*Decisiones,* XIV (1922), 294.

quick acquiescence to a comparatively reasonable command weakens the chance for a suspicion of a *grave* fear. This type of acquiescence is described by the classical phrase of Sanchez, *ut morem gerat.*[58]

The child has obeyed in consequence of a strong habit of accustomed obedience, and through the sense of dependence on his parents. Grave fear can hardly be alleged, even though the child would have acted differently if his parents had not commanded him to consent to the marriage.[59]

The combination of parental power and of accustomed obedience in the children seems to indicate that many marriages are entered into because of the children's accustomed obedience, or as the Rota expresses it, *morem ut gerat.*

The accustomed obedience of children is sometimes further influenced through the fatalism that is prevalent among the pagans and that still causes difficulties among the Catholics.[60] This fatalistic attitude was involved in a case that was sent to the Rota. It materially influenced the child to give consent, though he was very unwilling.[61] But whether the child had given consent under the influence of the specifically pagan concept of fatalism, or had merely resigned himself to the adverse set of circumstances in which he was placed, the grave fear connected with it could invalidate the marriage, even though the child should no longer have made external objections.[62]

It can happen then, that both accustomed obedience and a fatalistic attitude will be present in a given case. The accustomed obedience will lay the way open for qualified reverential fear coming from threats, harshness, etc., but the fatalistic attitude may cause a sudden end to objections by the child, who nevertheless remains very unwilling, and has not been released from the grave fear.

It sometimes happens that a child will threaten suicide in order to escape the unwanted marriage. This threat should not be con-

---

[58] *De Matrimonii Sacramento,* Lib. IV, disp. IX, n. 12.

[59] For a similar presentation of these principles, cf. a case not originating in China: *Decisiones,* XXIX (1937), 783—quoting Sanchez, *ut supra.*

[60] *Praxis Missionalis,* n. 163, 2°; Werner, *History,* I, 358.

[61] *Decisiones,* XVIII (1926), 158; *Decisiones,* XXI (1929), 108.

[62] Cf. a case from an unnamed diocese, *Decisiones,* XXVII (1935), 691.

sidered lightly, since the child, and especially the girl, may consider this as the only escape. The parties who make these threats may of course be without the intention of carrying them out, but suicide has sometimes been effected or at least attempted.[63]

Article 3. Engaged Parties

Among the customs governing engaged parties in China is that which demands that the engaged parties do not see each other during their engagement. This rule may obtain even up to the time for the wedding ceremony.[64]

Usually the parties are able at least to know each other's identity, and often may be well acquainted with each other. But if it has happened that they do not have any information about each other, their rights have been already transgressed in one matter, inasmuch as they have had no chance to give a proper consent to the engagement. As the time approaches for the marriage, the engaged parties are at a serious disadvantage, since they will have very little time to repudiate the engagement, and must face the prospect of the anger, etc., of their parents, without much time or opportunity to make a reasonable presentation of their objections. This of course presumes that they will intend to object, once they have gained sufficient knowledge of each other, and find that the proposed marriage will constitute a grave evil for them.

It should be noted that the custom of comparative seclusion of the prospective bride is on the wane. At present it seems that the engaged parties have a good, if not also an ample, opportunity to become informed about each other.[65]

Finally, there is a custom which obtains in parts of Central China,[66] and probably in other sections also, whereby the girl is expected to show extreme reluctance at the time she is to be taken by sedan chair to the home of her husband.[67]

---

63 *AAS,* IX (1917), 503; *Decisiones,* IX (1917), 24; also *Decisiones,* XIII (1921), 253.

64 *AAS,* IX (1917), 505; *Decisiones,* IX (1917), 26; also *Decisiones,* XVI (1924), 167; *Decisiones,* XVII (1925), 308-309.

65 Cf. Lin Yutang, *My Country and My People,* pp. 169-171, on the present emancipation of Chinese women.

66 The writer knows of this from personal observation.

67 The custom of "bringing home the bride" is widespread in China. Cf.

When the bride by her actions, sometimes quite violent, shows a reluctance toward being taken away in the sedan chair, these actions are to be interpreted as a purely external show of reluctance at being separated from her parents. The girl is giving an external indication of her filial piety. But no matter how hard or how long she struggles, she always gives up at an opportune moment, and is taken off triumphantly in the sedan chair to her new home. Obviously these actions cannot be interpreted as indicating that she was coerced into the marriage through force and fear. If the girl really intended to object to the marriage, she would choose another time, when her actions would not be wrongly interpreted.

Article 4. Summary

The observations of this chapter have been based mostly on Rota cases, which gave some illustrations of the influence of Chinese customs on marriage consent. These cases range from 1911 to 1930. The lack of cases, since 1930, from China and the adjacent countries with similar customs, makes it somewhat difficult to state with any assurance to what extent these customs are changing. The impact of Western customs has had some influence. But a thorough analysis of the present sociological changes in these countries is beyond the scope of this work. It seems correct and safe to say that the customs have changed somewhat in the larger, and especially the coastal cities, and that they have changed very little in the interior.

The discussions in this chapter on the parental power and the accustomed obedience of the children lead to the conclusion that force and fear *may easily* be used by the parents in forcing marriage on children who are unwilling. But the analysis of the parental power seems to indicate that their power is not much different from that of parents in countries where the Roman *patria potestas* is still in operation, though in a modified form. The power of Chinese parents is possibly stronger than, but hardly different in nature from, the modified *patria potestas* in other countries, e. g., in Europe.

Werner, *Sociology,* p. 27, col. 3, *in med.* quoting: "*China Review,* v. 204-205"; *AAS,* III (1911), 664; *Decisiones,* III (1911), 334. This case originated in Tonkin.

CONCLUSIONS

1. The phrase ***iniuste incussum*** in canon 1087 includes not only fear unjust in substance but also fear unjust in manner.[1]

2. It can be accepted as certain in practice that fear indirectly inflicted can invalidate a marriage.[2] However, many cases of fear indirectly inflicted are ultimately identifiable with cases of fear directly inflicted.[3]

3. Marriage causes which involve both fear and absolute physical force can be decided in favor of the nullity of the marriage even on the exclusive score or count of fear in abstraction from the score of physical force.[4]

4. *Patria potestas* as found in China and adjacent countries with similar customs is possibly a stronger power than, but not essentially different from, the modified form of *patria potestas* as found in some other countries. The principles on force and fear and reverential fear as enunciated in any Rota case can be applied with slight modifications to marriage cases in China.[5]

5. In China and adjacent countries, marriage engagements arranged by the parents for their children can easily offer an occasion for the infliction of force and fear as a means for coercing unwilling children into marriage.[6]

---

[1] See pp. 31-33, above.
[2] See pp. 33-45, above.
[3] See pp. 43-44, above.
[4] See pp. 22-25, above.
[5] See pp. 71-78, 84, above.
[6] See pp. 74-80, above.

Bibliography

SOURCES

Acta Apostolicae Sedis, Commentarium Officiale, Romae, 1909—.

Acta et Decreta Sacrorum Conciliorum Recentiorum, Collectio Lacensis, 7 vols., Friburgi Brisgoviae, 1870-1892.

Acta Sanctae Sedis, 41 vols., Romae, 1865-1908.

Bouscaren, T. Lincoln, *The Canon Law Digest,* 2 vols., Milwaukee: The Bruce Publishing Company, 1934-1943.

Bullarium Pontificium Sacrae Congregationis de Propaganda Fide, 8 vols., ed. S. Bayer, Romae, 1839-1858.

Canones et Decreta Sacrosancti Oecumenici Concilii Tridentini, Romae, 1882.

Civil Code of the Republic of China, The, translated by Chinglin Hsia, James L. E. Chow, Liu Chieh, Yukon Chang, Shanghai: Kelley and Walsh, 1931.

Codex Iuris Canonici Pii X Pontificis Maximi iussu digestus, Benedicti Papae XV auctoritate promulgatus, Romae: Typis Polyglottis Vaticanis, 1917; Reimpressio, 1933.

Codicis Iuris Canonici Fontes, cura Eñi Petri Card. Gasparri editi, 9 vols., Romae (postea Civitate Vaticana): Typis Polyglottis Vaticanis, 1923-1939 (Vols. VII, VIII et IX ed. cura et studio Eñi Iustiniani Card. Serédi).

Collectanea Constitutionum, Decretorum, Indultorum ac Instructionum Sanctae Sedis ad usum Operariorum Apostolicorum Societatis Missionum ad Exteros, Parisiis, 1880.

Corpus Iuris Canonici, ed. Lipsiensis secunda post Aemilii Ludovici Richteri curas . . . instruxit Aemilius Friedberg, 2 vols., Lipsiae, 1879-1881.

Corpus Iuris Civilis, 3 vols., Vol. I, ed. stereotypa quinta decima, *Institutiones* recognovit Paulus Kreuger, *Digesta* recognovit Theodorus Mommsen, retractavit Paulus Kreuger, Berolini: Apud Weidmannos, 1928.

Ius Pontificium de Propaganda Fide, ed. R. de Martinis, Pars prima, 7 vols. in 8, 1888-1897, Pars secunda vol. unic., 1909, Romae: Typographia Polyglotta S. C. de Propaganda Fide.

Pallottini, S., *Collectio omnium conclusionum, et resolutionum quae in causis propositis apud Sacram Congregationem Cardinalium S. Concilii Tridentini interpretum prodierunt ab eius institutione anno MDLXIV ad MDCCCLX, distinctis titulis alphabetico ordine per materias digesta,* 18 vols., Romae, 1868-1895.

Praxis Missionalis in Vicariatu Apostolico de Ichang, Wuchang: The Franciscan Press, 1935.

Primum Concilium Sinense, Anno 1924 . . . Celebratum: Acta—Decreta et Normae—Vota etc., Shanghai: Typographia Missionis Catholicae (T'ou-se-we), 1941.

S. Romanae Rotae Decisiones seu Sententiae quae . . . prodierunt anno 1909-1940, 32 vols., Romae: Typis Polyglottis Vaticanis, 1912-1949.

Schroeder, H. J., *Canons and Decrees of the Council of Trent,* St. Louis: Herder, 1941.

Thesaurus Resolutionum Sacrae Congregationis Concilii, 167 vols., Romae, 1718-1908.

Wadding, Lucas, *Annales Minorum seu Trium Ordinum a S. Francisco Institutorum,* 3. ed., 29 vols., Quaracchi, 1931-1948.

AUTHORS

Alphonsus Liguori, St., *Theologia Moralis,* ed. nova, cura et studio P. Leonardi Gaudé, 4 vols., Romae, 1905-1912.

Ayrinhac, H. A., *Marriage Legsilation in the New Code of Canon Law,* New York, 1918.

Bonaventure, St., *Opera Omnia,* 10 vols., in 11, Quaracchi, 1882-1902.

Blat, Albertus, *Commentarium Textus Codicis Iuris Canonici,* 5 vols. in 6, Vol. III (*De Rebus*), Pars I (*De Sacramentis*), 2. ed., Romae, 1924.

Bouscaren, T. Lincoln, and Ellis, Adam, *Canon Law, A Text and Commentary,* Milwaukee: The Bruce Publishing Company, 1946.

Cappello, Felix M., *Tractatus Canonico-Moralis de Sacramentis,* 3 vols. in 6, Vol. III, parts 1 and 2, *De Matrimonio,* 4. ed., Romae: Marietti, 1939.

Chelodi, Joannes-Ciprotti, Pius, *Ius Canonicum de Matrimonio et de Iudiciis Matrimonialibus,* 5. ed., Vicenza: Società Anonima Tipografica, 1947.

Coronata, Matthaeus, Conte a, *Institutiones Iuris Canonici,* 2. ed., 5 vols., Taurini: Marietti, 1939-1947.

———, *Institutiones Iuris Canonici, De Sacramentis,* 3 vols., Taurini, Marietti, 1943-1946.

Cosci, Christophorus, *De Separatione Tori Coniugalis,* folio ed., 2 vols., Romae, 1773-1779—and later ed., Lib. I and II only, 1 vol., Florentiae, 1856.

De Angelis, Philippus, *Praelectiones Iuris Canonici ad methodum Decretalium Gregorii IX exactae,* 5 vols. in 9, Romae, 1877-1891.

De Becker, Iulius, *De Matrimonio Praelectiones Canonicae,* ed. nova, Louvain: Ceuterick, 1931.

De Smet, Aloysius, *Tractatus Theologico-Canonicus de Sponsalibus et Matrimonio,* Romae, 1909, and 4. ed., Brugis, 1927.

Doheny, William, *Canonical Procedure in Matrimonial Cases,* 2 vols., Vol. I, 2. ed., 1948; Vol. II, 1944, Milwaukee: The Bruce Publishing Company.

Douglas, R., *Society in China,* London, 1894.

Escarra, Jean, *Le Droit Chinois,* Pekin: Editions Henri Vetch, 1936.

Ferraris, Lucius, *Prompta Bibliotheca Canonica, Iuridica, Moralis, Theologica, necnon Ascetica, Polemica, Rubricistica, Historica,* 9 vols., Romae, 1885-1899.

Frins, Victor, *De Actibus Humanis,* 2. ed., 2 vols., Friburgi Brisgoviae, 1897.

Gasparri, Petrus, *Tractatus Canonicus de Matrimonio,* ed. nova ad mentem Codicis I. C., 2 vols., Romae: Typis Polyglottis Vaticanis, 1932.

Genicot, E.-Salsmans, J., *Institutiones Theologiae Moralis,* 11. ed., 2 vols., Bruxellis, 1927.

Hostiensis (Henricus de Segusio), *In Quinque Decretalium Libros Commentaria,* 5 vols. in 3, Venetiis, 1581.

Juarez, S., *De Impedimento Matrimoniale Vis et Metus,* Murciae, 1928.

Lega, Michaelis, et Bartoccetti, Victorius, *Commentarius in Iudicia Ecclesiastica Iuxta Codicem Iuris Canonici,* 3 vols., Vols. I, II, Romae: Anonima Libraria Cattolica Italiana, 1938-1939; Vol. III, Romae: Editiones Comm. A. Arnodo, 1941.

Lin Yutang, *My Country and My People,* 2. ed., New York: John Day with Reynal and Hitchcock, 1938.

Lugo, Joannes de, *Disputationes de Iustitia et Iure,* 2. ed., 2 vols. in 1, Venetiis, 1751.

Merkelbach, Benedictus, *Summa Theologiae Moralis,* 3. ed., 3 vols., Parisiis: Descleè, 1939.

Ojetti, B., *Synopsis Rerum Moralium et Iuris Pontificii alphabetico ordine digesta,* 3. ed., 4 vols., Romae, 1909-1914.

Payen, G., *De Matrimonio in Missionibus ac potissimum in Sinis,* 2. ed., 3 vols., Zi-ka-wei: In Typographia T'ou-se-we, 1935-1936.

Petrovits, Joseph, *The New Church Law on Matrimony,* 2. ed., Philadelphia: McVey, 1926.

Pignatelli, Iacobus, *Consultationes Canonicae,* 9 vols. in 5, Coloniae Allobrogum, 1700, and supplement, Cosmopoli, 1711.

Pontius, Basilius, *De Sacramento Matrimonii,* 2. ed., Bruxellis, 1627.

Reiffenstuel, Anacletus, *Ius Canonicum Universum,* 5 vols. in 4, Monachii, 1702-1710.

——, *Tractatus de Regulis Juris,* Ingolstadii, 1733.

Roberti, Franciscus, *De Processibus,* 2. ed., third printing, Vol. I, Romae: Libraria Pontificii Instituti Utriusque Iuris, 1941.

——, *Codicis Iuris Canonici Schemata,* Lib. IV: *De Processibus,* I: *De Iudiciis in Genere,* In Civitate Vaticana: Typis Polyglottis Vaticanis, 1940.

Sanchez, Thomas, *Disputationum de Sancto Matrimonii Sacramento Libri Tres,* 3 vols., in 1, Antwerpiae, 1626.

Sangmeister, Joseph, *Force and Fear as Precluding Matrimonial Consent,* The Catholic University of America Canon Law Studies, n. 80, Washington, D. C.: The Catholic University of America, 1932.

Schmalzgrueber, Franciscus, *Jus Ecclesiasticum Universum,* 5 vols. in 12, Romae, 1843-1845.

Schmidlin, J.-Braun, M., *Catholic Mission History,* Techny: Mission Press, S. V. D., 1933.

Shiao-Tung Fei, *Peasant Life in China,* New York: Dutton and Co., 1939.

Thomas Aquinas, St., *Summa Theologica,* 6 vols., Taurini, Marietti, 1937.

——, *Opera Omnia,* 34 vols., Parisiis, 1871-1882.

Vermeersch, Arthurus, *Theologiae Moralis Principia, Responsa, Consilia,* 4 vols., Vol. III, Brugis, 1923.

Vermeersch, A.-Creusen, I, *Epitome Iuris Canonici,* 5. ed., 3 vols., Mechliniae-Romae, H. Dessain, 1933-1936.

Vlaming, Th., *Praelectiones Iuris Matrimonii ad Normam Codicis Iuris Canonici,* 3. ed., 2 vols., Bussum, 1919-1921.

Vromant, G., *Ius Missionariorum,* Tomus V, *De Matrimonio,* Louvain: Museum Lessianum, 1931.

Werner, E., *A History of Chinese Civilization,* ? vols., Vol. I, Shanghai: The Shanghai Times, 1940.

———, *Descriptive Sociology: Chinese,* London, 1910.

Wernz, F. X., *Ius Decretalium,* 3. ed., 6 vols. in 10, Prati, 1913-1915.

Wernz, F. X.-Vidal, P., *Ius Canonicum,* 7 vols. in 8, Romae: Universitas Gregoriana, 1923-1938; Vol. II, *De Personis,* 3. ed., recognovit P. Aguirre, 1942; Vol. V, *Ius Matrimoniale,* 3. ed., recognovit P. Aguirre, 1946.

Winslow, Francis, *A Commentary on the Apostolic Faculties,* New York: Field Afar Press, 1946.

Woywod, S.-Smith, C., *A Practical Commentary on the Code of Canon Law,* 2. ed., 2 vols., 10th printing, New York: Joseph Wagner, 1946.

ARTICLES

Ciprotti, Pio, "Iurisprudentia S. R. Rotae de metu reverentiali ex parentum iussu," *Appollinaris,* XIV (1941), 84-88.

Claeys Bouuaert F., "De metus influxu quoad valorem actuum et quoad delicta et poenas secundum Codicem Iuris Canonici," *Jus Pontificium,* VI (1926), 105-111; 138-144.

Roberti, Franciscus, "De metu indirecto quoad negotia iuridica praesertim matrimonium," *Apollinaris,* XI (1938), 557-561.

Rossi, J., "De consensu matrimoniali," *Analecta Ecclesiastica,* XVIII (1910), 350-363, 463-466; XIX (1911), 21-28, 67-74, 104-115, 181-191, 372-383.

Wyszynski, M., "Utrum metus indirecte incussus dirimere possit matrimonium," *Jus Pontificium,* X (1930), 193-200; XI (1931), 42-51; XII (1932), 43-52, 122-127; XIII (1933), 52-63—Dissertationes ex Ephemeridibus Jus Pontificium excerptae ac separatim editae, Series II, Fasc. XX, Romae: *Jus Pontificium,* 1933.

PERIODICALS

Analecta Ecclesiastica, Romae, 1893-1911.

Apollinaris, Romae, 1928—.

Jus Pontificium, Romae, 1921-1940.

Periodica de Re Canonica et Morali, Brugis, 1905—; ab anno 1927: *Periodica de Re Canonica, Morali, Liturgica,* Brugis (1927-1936) et Romae (1937—).

Abbreviations

AAS—*Acta Apostolicae Sedis.*

Decisiones—*S. Romanae Rotae Decisiones seu Sententiae.*

Fontes—*Codicis Iuris Canonici Fontes.*

Instr.—Instructio.

IP de PF—*Ius Pontificium de Propaganda Fide.*

Chronological Listing of the Rota Cases Cited in this Dissertation

III (1911), 332-340—S. R. R., *Tunkinen.* (Nullitatis Matrimonii), 7 iul. 1911, coram R. P. D. Francisco Heiner, Dec. XXX.

V (1913), 53-61—S. R. R., *Taikon* (Korea) (Nullitatis Matrimonii), 16 ian. 1913, coram R. P. D. Friderico Cattani Amadori, Dec. V.

IX (1917), 23-30—S. R. R., *Ce-li Centralis* (Nullitatis Matrimonii), 10 feb. 1917, coram R. P. D. Guilelmo Sebastianelli, Decano, Dec. III.

XI (1919), 170-178—S. R. R., Nullitatis Matrimonii, 14 nov. 1919, coram R. P. D. Ioanne Prior, Dec. XIX.

XIII (1921), 251-256—S. R. R., *Tonkin Orientalis* (Nullitatis Matrimonii), 18 aug. 1921, coram R. P. D. Friderico Cattani Amadori, Dec. XXVI.

XIV (1922), 1-13—S. R. R., Nullitatis Matrimonii, 9 ian. 1922, coram R. P. D. Iosepho Florczak, Dec. I.

XIV (1922), 78-82—S. R. R., Nullitatis Matrimonii, 31 mar. 1922, coram R. P. D. Maximo Massimi, Dec. IX.

XIV (1922), 290-298—S. R. R., *Ton-Kin Orient.* (Nullitatis Matrimonii), 14 aug. 1922, coram R. P. D. Friderico Cattani Amadori, Dec. XXXI.

XV (1923), 127-135—S. R. R., *Shan-si* (Nullitatis Matrimonii), 29 iun. 1923, coram R. P. D. Iosepho Florczak, Dec. XIV.

XVI (1924), 67-73—S. R. R., Nullitatis Matrimonii, 29 feb. 1924, coram R. P. D. Andrea Jullien, Dec. VIII.

XVI (1924), 126-138—S. R. R., Nullitatis Matrimonii, 8 apr. 1924, coram R. P. D. Ubaldo Mannucci, Dec. XVI.

XVI (1924), 138-144—S. R. R., *Tonkini Maritimi* (Nullitatis Matrimonii), 9 apr. 1924, coram R. P. D. Andrea Jullien, Dec. XVII.

XVI (1924), 163-172—S. R. R., Nullitatis Matrimonii, 30 mai. 1924, coram R. P. D. Ubaldo Mannucci, Dec. XX.

XVI (1924), 326-340—S. R. R., Nullitatis Matrimonii, 6 aug. 1924, coram R. P. D. Francisco Parrillo, Dec. XXXVII.

XVII (1925), 307-312—S. R. R., *Shangtung Merid.* (Nullitatis Matrimonii), 31 iul. 1925, coram R. P. D. Andrea Jullien, Dec. XL.

XVIII (1926), 93-102—S. R. R., Nullitatis Matrimonii, 24 mar. 1926, coram R. P. D. Francisco Parrillo, Dec. XII.

XVIII (1926), 151-158—S. R. R., *Luanfu* (Nullitatis Matrimonii), 20 apr. 1926, coram R. P. D. Francisco Guglielmi, Dec. XIX.

XVIII (1926), 213-221—S. R. R., *Chansi Meridionalis* (Nullitatis Matrimonii), 25 iun. 1926, coram R. P. D. Iulio Grazioli, Dec. XXVII.

XIX (1927), 256-261—S. R. R., Nullitatis Matrimonii, 2 iul. 1927, coram R. P. D. Maximo Massimi, Decano, Dec. XXXII.

XIX (1927), 404-415—S. R. R., *Ning-po* (Nullitatis Matrimonii), 10 aug. 1927, coram R. P. D. Henrico Quattrocolo, Dec. XLVI.

XX (1928), 272-281—S. R. R., Nullitatis Matrimonii, 30 iun. 1928, coram R. P. D. Maximo Massimi, Decano, Dec. XXX.

XX (1928), 363-368—S. R. R., *Transilvanien.* (Nullitatis Matrimonii), 4 aug. 1928, coram R. P. D. Maximo Massimi, Decano, Dec. XL.

XX (1928), 402-413—S. R. R., Nullitatis Matrimonii, 11 aug. 1928, coram R. P. D. Francisco Morano, Dec. XLVI.

XXI (1929), 104-111—S. R. R., *Ning-po* (Nullitatis Matrimonii), 18 feb. 1929, coram R. P. D. Ubaldo Mannucci, Dec. XII.

XXI (1929), 313-323—S. R. R., Nullitatis Matrimonii, 23 iul. 1929, coram R. P. D. Henrico Quattrocolo, Dec. XXXVII.

XXII (1930), 652-662—S. R. R., *Funing* (Nullitatis Matrimonii), 9 dec. 1930, coram R. P. D. Henrico Quattrocolo, Dec. LIX.

XXIII (1931), 11-18—S. R. R., *Alleppen.* (Nullitatis Matrimonii), 19 ian. 1931, coram R. P. D. Ubaldo Mannucci, Dec. II.

XXIII (1931), 413-423—S. R. R., *Aurelianen.* (Nullitatis Matrimonii), 11 aug. 1931, coram R. P. D. Arcturo Wynen, Dec. XLIX.

XXV (1933), 607-617—S. R. R., *Lincien.* (Nullitatis Matrimonii), 5 dec. 1933, coram R. P. D. Arcturo Wynen, Dec. LXXII.

XXVI (1934), 1-11—S. R. R., *Angelorum et S. Didaci* (Nullitatis Matrimonii), 4 ian. 1934, coram R. P. D. Guillelmo Heard, Dec. I.

XXVI (1934), 47-59—S. R. R., Nullitatis Matrimonii, 26 feb. 1934, coram R. P. D. Iulio Grazioli (et Maximo Massimi, Decano), Dec. VI.

XXVI (1934), 173-179—S. R. R., *Romana* (Nullitatis Matrimonii), 9 apr. 1934, coram R. P. D. Ubaldo Mannucci, Dec. XVII.

XXVI (1934), 225-230—S. R. R., *Corisopiten.* (Nullitatis Matrimonii), 25 apr. 1934, coram R. P. D. Maximo Massimi, Decano, Dec. XXIII.

XXVI (1934), 254-268—S. R. R., *Romana* (Nullitatis Matrimonii), 4 mai. 1934, coram R. P. D. Iulio Grazioli, Dec. XXVIII.

XXVI (1934), 563-570—S. R. R., *Turonen.* (Nullitatis Matrimonii), 2 aug. 1934, coram R. P. D. Arcturo Wynen, Dec. LXVII.

XXVI (1934), 663-671—S. R. R., *Berytcn. et Gibailen.* (Nullitatis Matrimonii), 20 oct. 1934, coram R. P. D.. Andrea Jullien, Dec. LXXVIII.

XXVI (1934), 718-726—S. R. R., *Vilnen.* (Nullitatis Matrimonii), 10 nov. 1934, coram R. P. D. Arcturo Wynen, Dec. LXXXIV.

XXVI (1934), 763-770—S. R. R., *Parisien.* (Nullitatis Matrimonii), 29 nov. 1934, coram R. P. D. Iulio Grazioli, Dec. XC.

XXVI (1934), 771-775—S. R. R., *Culmen.* (Nullitatis Matrimonii), 4 dec. 1934, coram R. P. D. Henrico Quattrocolo, Dec. XCI.

XXVI (1934), 781-785—S. R. R., Nullitatis Matrimonii, 17 dec. 1934, coram R. P. D. Ubaldo Mannucci, Dec. XCIII.

XXVII (1935), 69-75—S. R. R., *Mediolanen.* (Nullitatis Matrimonii), 18 feb. 1935, coram R. P. D. Ubaldo Mannucci, Dec. IX.

XXVII (1935), 212-215—S. R. R., *Tyrnavien.* (Nullitatis Matrimonii), 11 apr. 1935, coram R. P. D. Maximo Massimi, Decano, Dec. XXIV.

XXVII (1935), 274-280—S. R. R., Nullitatis Matrimonii, 29 apr. 1935, coram R. P. D. Maximo Massimi, Decano, Dec. XXXI.

XXVII (1935), 317-323—S. R. R., *Berolinen.* (Nullitatis Matrimonii), 25 mai. 1935, coram R. P. D. Arcturo Wynen, Dec. XXXVIII.

XXVII (1935), 402-414—S. R. R., Nullitatis Matrimonii, 10 iul. 1935, coram R. P. D. Maximo Massimi, Decano, Dec. XLVIII.

XXVII (1935), 690-694—S. R. R., Nullitatis Matrimonii, 21 dec. 1935, coram R. P. D. Arcturo Wynen, Dec. LXXXII.

XXVIII (1936), 87-91—S. R. R., *Oenipontana* (Nullitatis Matrimonii), 30 ian. 1936, coram R. P. D. Arcturo Wynen, Dec. IX.

XXVIII (1936), 181-188—S. R. R., *Westmonasterien.* (Nullitatis Matrimonii), 21 mar. 1936, coram R. P. D. Arcturo Wynen, Dec. XIX.

XXVIII (1936), 432-444—S. R. R., *Parisien.* (Nullitatis Matrimonii), 2 iul. 1936, coram R. P. D. Stanislao Janasik, Dec. XLVI.

XXVIII (1936), 469-478—S. R. R., *Matriten.* (Nullitatis Matrimonii), 11 iul. 1936, coram R. P. D. Arcturo Wynen, Dec. L.

XXVIII (1936), 496-503—S. R. R., *Romana* (Nullitatis Matrimonii), 14 iul. 1936, coram R. P. D. Alberto Canestri, Dec. LIII.

XXVIII (1936), 556-570—S. R. R., *Antiochen. Melchitarum* (Nullitatis Matrimonii), 5 aug. 1936, coram R. P. D. Iulio Grazioli, Decano, Dec. LIX.

XXVIII (1936), 629-634—S. R. R., *Tergestina* (Nullitatis Matrimonii), 22 oct. 1936, coram R. P. D. Arcturo Wynen, Dec. LXV.

XXVIII (1936), 642-651—S. R. R., *Mediolanen.* (Nullitatis Matrimonii), 31 oct. 1936, coram R. P. D. Andrea Jullien, Dec. LXVII.

XXVIII (1936), 658-666—S. R. R., *Romana* (Nullitatis Matrimonii), 9 nov. 1936, coram R. P. D. Alberto Canestri, Dec. LXIX.

XXVIII (1936), 674-680—S. R. R., *Placentina* (Nullitatis Matrimonii), 16 nov. 1936, coram R. P. D. Iulio Grazioli, Decano, Dec. LXXI.

XXVIII (1936), 702-713—S. R. R., *Beriten. Maronitarum* (Nullitatis Matrimonii), 26 nov. 1936, coram R. P. D. Iulio Grazioli, Decano, Dec. LXXIV.

XXVIII (1936), 713-718—S. R. R., Nullitatis Matrimonii, 28 nov. 1936, coram R. P. D. Andrea Jullien, Dec. LXXV.

XXIX (1937), 22-29—S. R. R., *Westmonasterien.* (Nullitatis Matrimonii), 16 ian. 1937, coram R. P. D. Andrea Jullien, Dec. IV.

XXIX (1937), 38-47—S. R. R., *Kielcen.* (Nullitatis Matrimonii), 21 ian. 1937, coram R. P. D. Iulio Grazioli, Decano, Dec. VI.

XXIX (1937), 69-76—S. R. R., *Ianuen.* (Nullitatis Matrimonii), 9 feb. 1937, coram R. P. D. Ioanne Teodori, Dec. IX.

XXIX (1937), 85-87—S. R. R., *Versalien.* (Nullitatis Matrimonii), 13 feb. 1937, coram R. P. D. Andrea Jullien, Dec. XI.

XXIX (1937), 214-226—S. R. R., *Messanen.* (Nullitatis Matrimonii), 16 mar. 1937, coram R. P. D. Arcturo Wynen, Dec. XIX.

XXIX (1937), 353-360—S. R. R., *Viennen.* (Quaerelae Nullitatis et Nullitatis Matrimonii), 22 mai. 1937, coram R. P. D. Alberto Canestri, Dec. XXXV.

XXIX (1937), 504-510—S. R. R., *Cassovien.* (Nullitatis Matrimonii), 12 iul. 1937, coram R. P. D. Andrea Jullien, Dec. L.

XXIX (1937), 601-616—S. R. R., *Antiochen. Melchitarum* (Nullitatis Matrimonii), 7 aug. 1937, coram R. P. D. Arcturo Wynen, Dec. LXI.
XXIX (1937), 782-793—S. R. R., *Romana* (Nullitatis Matrimonii), 22 dec. 1937, coram R. P. D. Andrea Jullien, Dec. LXXIX.
XXX (1938), 1-12—S. R. R., Nullitatis Matrimonii, 5 ian. 1938, coram R. P. D. Iulio Grazioli, Decano, Dec. I.
XXX (1938), 68-73—S. R. R., *Lublinen.* (Nullitatis Matrimonii), 24 ian. 1938, coram R. P. D. Guillelmo Heard, Dec. VII.
XXX (1938), 106-113—S. R. R., *Ceneten.* (Nullitatis Matrimonii), 16 feb. 1938, coram R. P. D. Arcturo Wynen, Dec. XII.
XXX (1938), 222-229—S. R. R., *Romana* (Nullitatis Matrimonii), 2 apr. 1938, coram R. P. D. Henrico Quattrocolo, Dec. XXIII.
XXX (1938), 248-262—S. R. R., *Taurinen.* (Nullitatis Matrimonii), 27 apr. 1938, coram R. P. D. Caesare Pecorari, Dec. XXVII.
XXX (1938), 369-381—S. R. R., Nullitatis Matrimonii, 30 iun. 1938, coram R. P. D. Iulio Grazioli, Dec. XLI..
XXX (1938), 381-394—S. R. R., Nullitatis Matrimonii, 5 iul 1938, coram R. P. D. Arcturo Wynen, Dec. XLII.
XXX (1938), 395-402—S. R. R., *Parisien.* (Nullitatis Matrimonii), 6 iul. 1938, coram R. P. D. Henrico Caiazzo, Dec. XLIII.
XXX (1938), 416-422—S. R. R., Nullitatis Matrimonii, 13 iun. 1938, coram R. P. D. Henrico Quattrocolo, Dec. XLV.
XXX (1938), 428-435—S. R. R., *Bononien.* (Nullitatis Matrimonii), 15 iul. 1938, coram R. P. D. Ioanne Teodori, Dec. XLVII.
XXX (1938), 435-451—S. R. R., Nullitatis Matrimonii, 20 iul. 1938, coram R. P. D. Caesare Pecorari, Dec. XLVIII.
XXX (1938), 640-646—S. R. R., *Romana* (Nullitatis Matrimonii), 30 nov. 1938, coram R. P. D. Henrico Quattrocolo, Dec. LXX.
XXX (1938), 646-658—S. R. R., Nullitatis Matrimonii, 30 nov. 1938, coram R. P. D. Caesare Pecorari, Dec. LXXI.
XXXI (1939), 19-24—S. R. R., *Neritonen.* (Nullitatis Matrimonii), 16 ian. 1939, coram R. P. D. Andrea Jullien, Dec. II.
XXXI (1939), 130-138—S. R. R., Nullitatis Matrimonii, 25 feb. 1939, coram R. P. D. Andrea Jullien, Dec. XVI.
XXXI (1939), 147-161—S. R. R., *Mediolanen.* (Nullitatis Matrimonii), 15 mar. 1939, coram R. P. D. Henrico Caiazzo, Dec. XVIII.
XXXI (1939), 192-204—S. R. R., *Parisien.* (Nullitatis Matrimonii), 13 apr. 1939, coram R. P. D. Iulio Grazioli, Decano, Dec. XXII.
XXXI (1939), 403-414—S. R. R., *Cracovien.* (Nullitatis Matrimonii), 10 iun. 1939, coram R. P. D. Stanislao Janasik, Dec. XLI.
XXXI (1939), 458-466—S. R. R., Nullitatis Matrimonii, 25 iul. 1939, coram R. P. D. Guillelmo Heard, Dec. XLVI.
XXXI (1939), 478-483—S. R. R., *Moguntina* (Nullitatis Matrimonii), 2 aug. 1939, coram R. P. D. Henrico Quattrocolo, Dec. XLVIII.
XXXI (1939), 521-534—S. R. R., *Strigonien.* (Nullitatis Matrimonii), 16 oct. 1939, coram R. P. D. Andrea Jullien, Dec. LII.
XXXI (1939), 560-572—S. R. R., *Romana* (Nullitatis Matrimonii), 29 nov. 1939, coram R. P. D. Henrico Caiazzo, Dec. LVI.

Alphabetical Index

Biographical Note

ROCH FRANCIS KNOPKE was born in Denver, Colorado, on August 22, 1906. After completing his elementary education at St. Elizabeth's School, he received his secondary education at Regis High School of the same city. He entered the Franciscan novitiate at Paterson in August, 1924, and made his simple profession there in August, 1925. Pursuing his philosophical and theological studies, he received the degree of Master of Arts from St. Bonaventure College, Allegany, N. Y., in June, 1930. He was ordained to the priesthood on June 7, 1931. In the following year, in June, he received the degree of Bachelor of Sacred Theology from the Catholic University of America. After thirteen years of work as a missionary assigned to the Prefecture Apostolic of Shasi, Hupeh, China, he enrolled in the School of Canon Law at the Catholic University of America in October, 1946, and received the Baccalaureate Degree in Canon Law in June, 1947, and the Licentiate Degree in Canon Law in June, 1948.

Canon Law Studies*

1. FRERIKS, REV. CELESTINE A., C.PP.S., J.C.D., Religious Congregations in Their External Relations, 121 pp., 1916.
2. GALLIHER, REV. DANIEL M., O.P., J.C.D., Canonical Elections, 117 pp., 1917.
3. BORKOWSKI, REV. AURELIUS L., O.F.M., J.C.D., De Confraternitatibus Ecclesiasticis, 136 pp., 1918.
4. CASTILLO, REV. CAYO, J.C.D., Disertación Historico-Canonica sobre la Potestad del Cabildo en Sede Vacante o Impedida del Vicario Capitular, 99 pp., 1919 (1918).
5. KUBELBECK, REV. WILLIAM J., S.T.B., J.C.D., The Sacred Penitentiaria and Its Relation to Faculties of Ordinaries and Priests, 129 pp., 1918.
6. PETROVITS, REV. JOSEPH, J.C., S.T.D., J.C.D., The New Church Law on Matrimony, X-461 pp., 1919.
7. HICKEY, REV. JOHN J., S.T.B., J.C.D., Irregularities and Simple Impediments in the New Code of Canon Law, 100 pp., 1920.
8. KLEKOTKA, REV. PETER J., S.T.B., J.C.D., Diocesan Consultors, 179 pp., 1920.
9. WANENMACHER, REV. FRANCIS, J.C.D., The Evidence in Ecclesiastical Procedure Affecting the Marriage Bond, 1920 (Printed 1935).
10. GOLDEN, REV. HENRY FRANCIS, J.C.D., Parochial Benefices in the New Code, IV-119 pp., 1921 (Printed 1925).
11. KOUDELKA, REV. CHARLES J., J.C.D., Pastors, Their Rights and Duties According to the New Code of Canon Law, 211 pp., 1921.
12. MELO, REV. ANTONIUS, O.F.M., J.C.D., De Exemptione Regularium, X-188 pp., 1921.
13. SCHAAF, REV. VALENTINE THEODORE, O.F.M., S.T.B., J.C.D., The Cloister, X-180 pp., 1921.
14. BURKE, REV. THOMAS JOSEPH, S.T.D., J.C.D., Competence in Ecclesiastical Tribunals, IV-117 pp., 1922.
15. LEECH, REV. GEORGE LEO, J.C.D., A Comparative Study of the Constitution "Apostolicae Sedis" and the "Codex Juris Canonici," 179 pp., 1922.
16. MOTRY, REV. HUBERT LOUIS, S.T.D., J.C.D., Diocesan Faculties According to the Code of Canon Law, II-167 pp., 1922.
17. MURPHY, REV. GEORGE LAWRENCE, J.C.D., Delinquencies and Penalties in the Administration and the Reception of the Sacraments, IV-121 pp., 1923.
18. O'REILLY, REV. JOHN ANTHONY, S.T.B., J.C.D., Ecclesiastical Sepulture in the New Code of Canon Law, II-129 pp., 1923.

*All published numbers are available from the Catholic University of America Press, 620 Michigan Avenue, N. E., Washington 17, D. C., except the following: nos. 1-114 inclusive, 116, 118, 120, 121, 122, 123, 136, 153, 162, 182, and 198. But the following numbers, now reissued, are obtainable from *The Jurist*, The Catholic University of America, Washington 17, D. C., namely: nos. 5, 7, 11, 17, 18, 19, 26, 28, 30, 31, 34, 42, 44, 51, 52 and 61.

19. MICHALICKA, REV. WENCESLAS CYRILL, O.S.B., J.C.D., Judicial Procedure in Dismissal of Clerical Exempt Religious, 107 pp., 1923.
20. DARGIN, REV. EDWARD VINCENT, S.T.B., J.C.D., Reserved Cases According to the Code of Canon Law, IV-103 pp., 1924.
21. GODFREY, REV. JOHN A., S.T.B., J.C.D., The Right of Patronage According to the Code of Canon Law, 153 pp., 1924.
22. HAGEDORN, REV. FRANCIS EDWARD, J.C.D., General Legislation on Indulgences, II-154 pp., 1924.
23. KING, REV. JAMES IGNATIUS, J.C.D., The Administration of the Sacraments to Dying Non-Catholics, V-141 pp., 1924.
24. WINSLOW, REV. FRANCIS JOSEPH, M.M., J.C.D., Vicars and Prefects Apostolic, IV-149 pp., 1924.
25. CORREA, REV. JOSE SERVELION, S.T.L., J.C.D., La Potestad Legislativa de la Iglesia Catolica, IV-127 pp., 1925.
26. DUGAN, REV. HENRY FRANCIS, A.M., J.C.D., The Judiciary Department of the Diocesan Curia, 87 pp., 1925.
27. KELLER, REV. CHARLES FREDERICK, S.T.B., J.C.D., Mass Stipends, 167 pp., 1925.
28. PASCHANG, REV. JOHN LINUS, J.C.D., The Sacramentals According to the Code of Canon Law, 129 pp., 1925.
29. PIONTEK, REV. CYRILLUS, O.F.M., S.T.B., J.C.D., De Indulto Exclaustrationis necnon Saecularizationis, XIII-289 pp., 1925.
30. KEARNEY, REV. RICHARD JOSEPH, S.T.B., J.C.D., Sponsors at Baptism According to the Code of Canon Law, IV-127 pp., 1925.
31. BARTLETT, REV. CHESTER JOSEPH, A.M., LL.B., J.C.D., The Tenure of Parochial Property in the United States of America, V-108 pp., 1926.
32. KILKER, REV. ADRIAN JEROME, J.C.D., Extreme Unction, V-425 pp., 1926.
33. MCCORMICK, REV. ROBERT EMMETT, J.C.D., Confessors of Religious, VIII-266 pp., 1926.
34. MILLER, REV. NEWTON THOMAS, J.C.D., Founded Masses According to the Code of Canon Law, VII-93 pp., 1926.
35. ROELKER, REV. EDWARD G., S.T.D., J.C.D., Principles of Privilege According to the Code of Canon Law, XI-166 pp., 1926.
36. BAKALARCZYK, REV. RICHARDUS, M.I.C., J.U.D., De Novitiatu, VIII-208 pp., 1927.
37. PIZZUTI, REV. LAWRENCE, O.F.M., J.U.L., De Parochis Religiosis, 1927. (Not Printed.)
38. BLILEY, REV. NICHOLAS MARTIN, O.S.B., J.C.D., Altars According to the Code of Canon Law, XIX-132 pp., 1927.
39. BROWN, MR. BRENDAN FRANCIS, A.B., LL.M., J.U.D., The Canonical Juristic Personality with Special References to its Status in the United States of America, V-212 pp., 1927.
40. CAVANAUGH, REV. WILLIAM THOMAS, C.P., J.U.D., The Reservation of the Blessed Sacrament, VIII-101 pp., 1927.
41. DOHENY, REV. WILLIAM J., C.S.C., A.B., J.U.D., Church Property: Modes of Acquisition, X-118 pp., 1927.

42. Feldhaus, Rev. Aloysius H., C.PP.S., J.C.D., Oratories, IX-141 pp., 1927.
43. Kelly, Rev. James Patrick, A.B., J.C.D., The Jurisdiction of the Simple Confessor, X-208 pp., 1927.
44. Neuberger, Rev. Nicholas J., J.C.D., Canon 6 or the Relation of the Codex Juris Canonici to the Preceding Legislation, V-95 pp., 1927.
45. O'Keefe, Rev. Gerald Michael, J.C.D., Matrimonial Dispensations, Powers of Bishops, Priests, and Confessors, VIII-232 pp., 1927.
46. Quigley, Rev. Joseph A. M., A.B., J.C.D., Condemned Societies, 139 pp., 1927.
47. Zaplotnik, Rev. Johannes Leo, J.C.D., De Vicariis Foraneis, X-142 pp., 1927.
48. Duskie, Rev. John Aloysius, A.B., J.C.D., The Canonical Status of the Orientals in the United States, VIII-196 pp., 1928.
49. Hyland, Rev. Francis Edward, J.C.D., Excommunication, Its Nature, Historical Development and Effects, VIII-181 pp., 1928.
50. Reinmann, Rev. Gerald Joseph, O.M.C., J.C.D., The Third Order Secular of Saint Francis, 201 pp., 1928.
51. Schenk, Rev. Francis J., J.C.D., The Matrimonial Impediments of Mixed Religion and Disparity of Cult, XVI-318 pp., 1929.
52. Coady, Rev. John Joseph, S.T.D., J.U.D., A.M., The Appointment of Pastors, VIII-150 pp., 1929.
53. Kay, Rev. Thomas Henry, J.C.D., Competence in Matrimonial Procedure, VIII-164 pp., 1929.
54. Turner, Rev. Sidney Joseph, C.P., J.U.D., The Vow of Poverty, XLIX-217 pp., 1929.
55. Kearney, Rev. Raymond A., A.B., S.T.D., J.C.D., The Principles of Delegation, VII-149 pp., 1929.
56. Conran, Rev. Edward James, A.B., J.C.D., The Interdict, V-163 pp., 1930.
57. O'Neill, Rev. William H., J.C.D., Papal Rescripts of Favor, VII-218 pp., 1930.
58. Bastnagel, Rev. Clement Vincent, J.U.D., The Appointment of Parochial Adjutants and Assistants, XV-257 pp., 1930.
59. Ferry, Rev. William A., A.B., J.C.D., Stole Fees, V-136 pp., 1930.
60. Costello, Rev. John Michael, A.B., J.C.D., Domicile and Quasi-Domicile, VII-201 pp., 1930.
61. Kremer, Rev. Michael Nicholas, A.B., S.T.B., J.C.D., Church Support in the United States, VI-136 pp., 1930.
62. Angulo, Rev. Luis, C.M., J.C.D., Legislación de la Iglesia sobre la intención en la aplicación de la Santa Misa, VII-104 pp., 1931.
63. Frey, Rev. Wolfgang Norbert, O.S.B., A.B., J.C.D., The Act of Religious Profession, VIII-174 pp., 1931.
64. Roberts, Rev. James Brendan, A.B., J.C.D., The Banns of Marriage, XIV-140 pp., 1931.
65. Ryder, Rev. Raymond Aloysius, A.B., J.C.D., Simony, IX-151 pp., 1931.

66. Campagna, Rev. Angelo, Ph.D., J.U.D., Il Vicario Generale del Vescovo, VII-205 pp., 1931.
67. Cox, Rev. Joseph Godfrey, A.B., J.C.D., The Administration of Seminaries, VI-124 pp., 1931.
68. Gregory, Rev. Donald J., J.U.D., The Pauline Privilege, XV-165 pp., 1931.
69. Donohue, Rev. John F., J.C.D., The Impediment of Crime, VII-110 pp., 1931.
70. Dooley, Rev. Eugene A., O.M.I., J.C.D., Church Law on Sacred Relics, IX-143 pp., 1931.
71. Orth, Rev. Clement Raymond, O.M.C., J.C.D., The Approbation of Religious Institutes, 171 pp., 1931.
72. Pernicone, Rev. Joseph M., A.B., J.C.D., The Ecclesiastical Prohibition of Books, XII-267 pp., 1932.
73. Clinton, Rev. Connell, A.B., J.C.D., The Paschal Precept, IX-108 pp., 1932.
74. Donnelly, Rev. Francis B., A.M., S.T.L., J.C.D., The Diocesan Synod, VIII-125 pp., 1932.
75. Torrente, Rev. Camilo, C.M.F., J.C.D., Las Procesiones Sagradas, V-145 pp., 1932.
76. Murphy, Rev. Edwin J., C.PP.S., J.C.D., Suspension Ex Informata Conscientia, XI-122 pp., 1932.
77. MacKenzie, Rev. Eric F., A.M., S.T.L., J.C.D., The Delict of Heresy in its Commission, Penalization, Absolution, VII-124 pp., 1932.
78. Lyons, Rev. Avitus E., S.T.B., J.C.D., The Collegiate Tribunal of First Instance, XI-147 pp., 1932.
79. Connolly, Rev. Thomas A., J.C.D., Appeals, XI-195 pp., 1932.
80. Sangmeister, Rev. Joseph V., A.B., J.C.D., Force and Fear as Precluding Matrimonial Consent, V-211 pp., 1932.
81. Jaeger, Rev. Leo A., A.B., J.C.D., The Administration of Vacant and Quasi-Vacant Episcopal Sees in the United States, IX-229 pp., 1932.
82. Rimlinger, Rev. Herbert T., J.C.D., Error Invalidating Matrimonial Consent, VII-79 pp., 1932.
83. Barrett, Rev. John D. M., SS., J.C.D., A Comparative Study of the Councils of Baltimore and the Code of Canon Law, X-223 pp., 1932.
84. Carberry, Rev. John J., Ph.D., S.T.D., J.C.D., The Juridical Form of Marriage, X-177 pp., 1934.
85. Dolan, Rev. John L., A.B., J.C.D., The Defensor Vinculi, XII-157 pp., 1934.
86. Hannan, Rev. Jerome D., A.M., S.T.D., LL.B., J.C.D., The Canon Law of Wills, IX-517 pp., 1934.
87. Lemieux, Rev. Delisle A., A.M., J.C.D., The Sentence in Ecclesiastical Procedure, IX-131, pp., 134.
88. O'Rourke, Rev. James J., A.B., J.C.D., Parish Registers, VII-109 pp., 1934.
89. Timlin, Rev. Bartholomew, O.F.M., A.M., J.C.D., Conditional Matrimonial Consent, X-381 pp., 1934.

90. WAHL, REV. FRANCIS X., A.B., J.C.D., The Matrimonial Impediments of Consanguinity and Affinity, VI-125 pp., 1934.
91. WHITE, REV. ROBERT J., A.B., LL.B., S.T.B., J.C.D., Canonical Ante-Nuptial Promises and the Civil Law, VI-152 pp., 1934.
92. HERRERA, REV. ANTONIO PARRA, O.C.D., J.C.D., Legislación Eclesiástica sobra el Ayuno y la Abstinencia, XI-191 pp., 1935.
93. KENNEDY, REV. EDWIN J., J.C.D., The Special Matrimonial Process in Cases of Evident Nullity, X-165 pp., 1935.
94. MANNING, REV. JOHN J., A.B., J.C.D., Presumption of Law in Matrimonial Procedure, XI-111 pp., 1935.
95. MOEDER, REV. JOHN M., J.C.D., The Proper Bishop for Ordination and Dismissorial Letters, VII-135 pp., 1935.
96. O'MARA, REV. WILLIAM A., A.B., J.C.D., Canonical Causes for Matrimonial Dispensations, IX-155 pp., 1935.
97. REILLY, REV. PETER, J.C.D., Residence of Pastors, IX-81 pp., 1935.
98. SMITH, REV. MARINER T., O.P., S.T.Lr., J.C.D., The Penal Law for Religious, VII-169 pp., 1935.
99. WHALEN, REV. DONALD W., A.M., J.C.D., The Value of Testimonial Evidence in Matrimonial Procedure, XIII-297 pp., 1935.
100. CLEARY, REV. JOSEPH F., J.C.D., Canonical Limitations on the Alienation of Church Property, VIII-141 pp., 1936.
101. GLYNN, REV. JOHN C., J.C.D., The Promoter of Justice, XX-337 pp., 1936.
102. BRENNAN, REV. JAMES H., S.S., M.A., S.T.B., J.C.D., The Simple Convalidation of Marriage, VI-135 pp., 1937.
103. BRUNINI, REV. JOSEPH BERNARD, J.C.D., The Clerical Obligations of Canons 139 and 142, X-121 pp., 1937.
104. CONNOR, REV. MAURICE, A.B., J.C.D., The Administrative Removal of Pastors, VIII-159 pp., 1937.
105. GUILFOYLE, REV. MERLIN JOSEPH, J.C.D., Custom, XI-144 pp., 1937.
106. HUGHES, REV. JAMES AUSTIN, A.B., A.M., J.C.D., Witnesses in Criminal Trials of Clerics, IX-140 pp., 1937.
107. JANSEN, REV. RAYMOND J., A.B., S.T.L., J.C.D., Canonical Provisions for Catechetical Instruction, VII-153 pp., 1937.
108. KEALY, REV. JOHN JAMES, A.B., J.C.D., The Introductory Libellus in Church Court Procedure, XI-121 pp., 1937.
109. MCMANUS, REV. JAMES EDWARD, C.SS.R., J.C.D., The Administration of Temporal Goods in Religious Institutes, XVI-196 pp., 1937.
110. MORIARTY, REV. EUGENE JAMES, J.C.D., Oaths in Ecclesiastical Courts, X-115 pp., 1937.
111. RAINER, REV. ELIGIUS GEORGE, C.SS.R., J.C.D., Suspension of Clerics, XVII-249 pp., 1937.
112. REILLY, REV. THOMAS F., C.SS.R., J.C.D., Visitation of Religious, VI-195 pp., 1938.
113. MORIARTY, REV. FRANCIS E., C.SS.R., J.C.D., The Extraordinary Absolution from Censures, XV-334 pp., 1938.

114. CONNOLLY, REV. NICHOLAS P., J.C.D., The Canonical Erection of Parishes, X-132 pp., 1938.
115. DONOVAN, REV. JAMES JOSEPH, J.C.D., The Pastor's Obligation in Prenuptial Investigation, XII-322 pp., 1938.
116. HARRIGAN, REV. ROBERT J., M.A., S.T.B., J.C.D., The Radical Sanation of Invalid Marriages, VIII-208 pp., 1938.
117. BOFFA, REV. CONRAD HUMBERT, J.C.D., Canonical Provisions for Catholic Schools, VII-211 pp., 1939.
118. PARSONS, REG. ANSCAR JOHN, O.M.Cap., J.C.D., Canonical Elections, XII-236 pp., 1939.
119. REILLY, REV. EDWARD MICHAEL, A.B., J.C.D., The General Norms of Dispensation, XII-156 pp., 1939.
120. RYAN, REV. GERALD ALOYSIUS, A.B., J.C.D., Principles of Episcopal Jurisdiction, XII-172 pp., 1939.
121. BURTON, REV. FRANCIS JAMES, C.S.C., A.B., J.C.D., A Commentary on Canon 1125, X-222 pp., 1940.
122. MIASKIEWICZ, REV. FRANCIS SIGISMUND, J.C.D., Supplied Jurisdiction According to Canon 209, XII-340 pp., 1940.
123. RICE, REV. PATRICK WILLIAM, A.B., J.C.D., Proof of Death in Prenuptial Investigation, VIII-156 pp., 1940.
124. ANGLIN, REV. THOMAS FRANCIS, M.S., J.C.D., The Eucharistic Fast, VIII-183 pp., 1941.
125. COLEMAN, REV. JOHN JEROME, J.C.D., The Minister of Confirmation, VI-153 pp., 1941.
126. DOWNS, REV. JOHN EMMANUEL, A.B., J.C.D., The Concept of Clerical Immunity, XI-163 pp., 1941.
127. ESSWEIN, REV. ANTHONY ALBERT, J.C.D., Extrajudicial Penal Powers of Ecclesiastical Superiors, X-144 pp., 1941.
128. FARRELL, REV. BENJAMIN FRANCIS, M.A., S.T.L., J.C.D., The Rights and Duties of the Local Ordinary Regarding Congregations of Women Religious of Pontifical Approval, V-195 pp., 1941.
129. FEENEY, REV. THOMAS JOHN, A.B., S.T.L., J.C.D., Restitutio in Integrum, VI-169 pp., 1941.
130. FINDLAY, REV. STEPHEN WILLIAM, O.S.B., A.B., J.C.D., Canonical Norms Governing the Deposition and Degradation of Clerics, XVII-279 pp., 1941.
131. GOODWINE, REV. JOHN, A.B., S.T.L., J.C.D., The Right of the Church to Acquire Property, VIII-119 pp., 1941.
132. HESTON, REV. EDWARD LOUIS, C.S.C., PH.D., S.T.D., J.C.D., The Alienation of Church Property in the United States, XII-222 pp., 1941.
133. HOGAN, REV. JAMES JOHN, A.B., S.T.L., J.C.D., Judicial Advocates and Procurators, XIII-200 pp., 1941.
134. KEALY, REV. THOMAS M., A.B., LITT.B., J.C.D., Dowry of Women Religious, IX-152 pp., 1941.
135. KEENE, REV. MICHAEL JAMES, O.S.B., J.C.D., Religious Ordinaries and Canon 198, V-164 pp., 1941. (Printed, 1942).

136. Kerin, Rev. Charles A., S.S., M.A., S.T.B., J.C.D., The Privation of Christian Burial, XVI-279 pp., 1941.
137. Louis, Rev. William Francis, M.A., J.C.D., Diocesan Archives, X-101 pp., 1941.
138. McDevitt, Rev. Gilbert Joseph, A.B., J.C.D., Legitimacy and Legitimation, X-247 pp., 1941.
139. McDonough, Rev. Thomas Joseph, A.B., J.C.D., Apostolic Administrators, X-217 pp., 1941.
140. Meier, Rev. Carl Anthony, A.B., J.C.D., Penal Administrative Procedure Against Negligent Pastors, XI-240 pp., 1941.
141. Schmidt, Rev. John Rogg, A.B., J.C.D., The Principles of Authentic Interpretation in Canon 17 of the Code of Canon Law, XII-331 pp., 1941.
142. Slafkosky, Rev. Andrew Leonard, A.B., J.C.D., The Canonical Episcopal Visitation of the Diocese, X-197 pp., 1941.
143. Swoboda, Rev. Innocent Robert, O.F.M., J.C.D., Ignorance in Relation to the Imputability of Delicts, IX-271 pp., 1941.
144. Dubé, Rev. Arthur Joseph, A.B., J.C.D., The General Principles for the Reckoning of Time in Canon Law, VIII-299 pp., 1941.
145. McBride, Rev. James T., A.B., J.C.D., Incardination and Excardination of Seculars, XX-585 pp., 1941.
146. Krol, Rev. John T., J.C.D., The Defendant in Ecclesiastical Trials, XII-207 pp., 1942.
147. Comyns, Rev. Joseph J., C.SS.R., A.B., J.C.D., Papal and Episcopal Administration of Church Property, XIV-155 pp., 1942.
148. Barry, Rev. Garrett Francis, O.M.I., J.C.D., Violation of the Cloister, XII-260 pp., 1942.
149. Bolduc, Rev. Gatien, C.S.V., A.B., S.T.L., J.C.D., Les Etudes dans les Religions Cléricales, VIII-155 pp., 1942.
150. Boyle, Rev. David John, M.A., J.C.D., The Juridic Effects of Moral Certitude on Pre-Nuptial Guarantees, XII-188 pp., 1942.
151. Canavan, Rev. Walter Joseph, M.A., Litt.D., J.C.D., The Profession of Faith, XII-143 pp., 1942.
152. Desrochers, Rev. Bruno, A.B., Ph.L., S.T.B., J.C.D., Le Premier Concile Plénier de Québec et le Code de Droit Canonique, XIV-186 pp., 1942.
153. Dillon, Rev. Robert Edward, A.B., J.C.D., Common Law Marriage, X-148 pp., 1942.
154. Dodwell, Rev. Edward John, Ph.D., S.T.B., J.C.D., The Time and Place for the Celebration of Marriage, X-156 pp., 1942.
155. Donnellan, Rev. Thomas Andrew, A.B., J.C.D., The Obligation of the Missa pro Populo, VII-131 pp., 1942.
156. Eltz, Rev. Louis Anthony, A.B., J.C.D., Cooperation in Crime, XII-208 pp., 1942.
157. Gass, Rev. Sylvester Francis, M.A., J.C.D., Ecclesiastical Pensions, XI-206 pp., 1942.

158. GUINIVEN, REV. JOHN JOSEPH, C.SS.R., J.C.D., The Precept of Hearing Mass, XIV-188 pp., 1942.
159. GULCZYNSKI, REV. JOHN THEOPHILUS, J.C.D., The Desecration and Violation of Churches, X-126 pp., 1942.
160. HAMMILL, REV. JOHN LEO, M.A., J.C.D., The Obligations of the Traveler According to Canon 14, VIII-204 pp., 1942.
161. HAYDT, REV. JOHN JOSEPH, A.B., J.C.D., Reserved Benefices, XI-148 pp., 1942.
162. HUSER, REV. ROGER JOHN, O.F.M., A.B., J.C.D., The Crime of Abortion in Canon Law, XII-187 pp., 1942.
163. KEARNEY, REV. FRANCIS PATRICK, A.B., S.T.L., J.C.D., The Principles of Canon 1127, X-162 pp., 1942.
164. LINAHEN, REV. LEO JAMES, S.T.L., J.C.D., De Absolutione Complicis in Peccato Turpi, V-114 pp., 1942.
165. MCCLOSKEY, REV. JOSEPH ALOYSIUS, A.B., J.C.D., The Subject of Ecclesiastical Law According to Canon 12, XVII-246 pp., 1942. (Printed, 1943).
166. O'NEILL, REV. FRANCIS JOSEPH, C.SS.R., J.C.D., The Dismissal of Religious in Temporary Vows, VIII-220 pp., 1942.
167. PRINCE, REV. JOHN EDWARD, A.B., S.T.B., J.C.D., The Diocesan Chancellor, X-136 pp., 1942.
168. RIESNER, REV. ALBERT JOSEPH, C.SS.R., J.C.D., Apostates and Fugitives from Religious Institutes, IX-168 pp., 1942.
169. STENGER, REV. JOSEPH BERNARD, J.C.D., The Mortgaging of Church Property, 186 pp., 1942.
170. WALDRON, REV. JOSEPH FRANCIS, A.B., J.C.D., The Minister of Baptism, XII-197 pp., 1942.
171. WILLETT, REV. ROBERT ALBERT, J.C.D., The Probative Value of Documents in Ecclesiastical Trials, X-124 pp., 1942.
172. WOEBER, REV. EDWARD MARTIN, M.A., J.C.D., The Interpellations, XII-161 pp., 1942.
173. BENKO, REV. MATTHEW ALOYSIUS, O.S.B., M.A., J.C.D., The Abbot *Nullius*, XVI-148 pp., 1943.
174. CHRIST, REV. JOSEPH JAMES, M.A., S.T.L., J.C.D., Dispensation from Vindicative Penalties, XIV-285 pp., 1943.
175. CLANCY, REV. PATRICK M. J., O.P., A.B., S.T.LR., J.C.D., The Local Religious Superior, X-229 pp., 1943.
176. CLARKE, REV. THOMAS JAMES, J.C.D., Parish Societies, XII-147 pp., 1943.
177. CONNOLLY, REV. JOHN PATRICK, S.T.L., J.C.D., Synodal Examiners and Parish Priest Consultors, X-223 pp., 1943.
178. DRUMM, REV. WILLIAM MARTIN, A.B., J.C.D., Hospital Chaplains, XII-175 pp., 1943.
179. FLANAGAN, REV. BERNARD JOSEPH, A.B., S.T.L., J.C.D., The Canonical Erection of Religious Houses, X-147 pp., 1943.
180. KELLEHER, REV. STEPHEN JOSEPH, A.B., S.T.B., J.C.D., Discussions with Non-Catholics: Canonical Legislation, X-93 pp., 1943.

181. LEWIS, REV. GORDIAN, C.P., J.C.D., Chapters in Religious Institutes, XII-169 pp., 1943.
182. MARX, REV. ADOLPH, J.C.D., The Declaration of Nullity of Marriages Contracted Outside the Church, X-151 pp., 1943.
183. MATULENAS, REV. RAYMOND ANTHONY, O.S.B., A.B., J.C.D., Communication, a Source of Privileges, XII-225 pp., 1943.
184. O'LEARY, REV. CHARLES GERARD, C.SS.R., J.C.D., Religious Dismissed After Perpetual Profession, X-213 pp., 1943.
185. POWER, REV. CORNELIUS MICHAEL, J.C.D., The Blessing of Cemeteries, XII-231 pp., 1943.
186. SHUHLER, REV. RALPH VINCENT, O.S.A., J.C.D., Privileges of Religious to Absolve and Dispense, XII-195 pp., 1943.
187. ZIOLKOWSKI, REV. THADDEUS STANISLAUS, A.B., J.C.D., The Consecration and Blessing of Churches, XII-151 pp., 1943.
188. HENEGHAN, REV. JOHN JOSEPH, S.T.D., J.C.D., The Marriages of Unworthy Catholics: Canons 1065 and 1066, XVI-213 pp., 1944.
189. CARROLL, REV. COLEMAN FRANCIS, M.A., S.T.L., J.C.L., Charitable Institutions.
190. CIESLUK, REV. JOSEPH EDWARD, PH.B., S.T.L., J.C.D., National Parishes in the United States, VI-178 pp., 1944.
191. COBURN, REV. VINCENT PAUL, A.B., J.C.D., Marriages of Conscience, XII-172 pp., 1944.
192. CONNORS, REV. CHARLES PAUL, C.S.SP., A.B., J.C.D., Extra-Judicial Procurators in the Code of Canon Law, X-94 pp., 1944.
193. COYLE, REV. PAUL RAYMOND, A.B., J.C.D., Judicial Exceptions, X-142 pp., 1944.
194. FAIR, REV. BARTHOLOMEW FRANCIS, A.B., S.T.L., J.C.D., The Impediment of Abduction, XII-122 pp., 1944.
195. GALLAGHER, REV. THOMAS RAPHAEL, O.P., A.B., S.T.LR., J.C.D., The Examination of the Qualities of the Ordinand, X-166 pp., 1944.
196. GANNON, REV. JOHN MARK, S.T.L., J.C.D., The Interstices Required for the Promotion to Orders, XII-100 pp., 1944.
197. GOLDSMITH, REV. J. WILLIAM, B.C.S., S.T.L., J.C.D., The Competence of Church and State Over Marriages—Disputed Points, X-128 pp., 1944.
198. GOODWINE, REV. JOSEPH GERARD, A.B., S.T.B., J.C.D., The Reception of Converts, XIV-326 pp., 1944.
199. KOWALSKI, REV. ROMUALD EUGENE, O.F.M., A.B., J.C.D., Sustenance of Religious Houses of Regulars, X-174 pp., 1944.
200. McCOY, REV. ALAN EDWARD, O.F.M., J.C.D., Force and Fear in Relation to Delictual Imputability and Penal Responsibility, XII-160 pp., 1944.
201. McDEVITT, REV. VINCENT JOHN, PH.B., S.T.L., J.C.L., Perjury.
202. MARTIN, REV. THOMAS OWEN, PH.D., S.T.D., J.C.D., Adverse Possession, Prescription and Limitation of Actions: The Canonical "Praescriptio," XX-208 pp., 1944.

203. MIKLOSOVIC, REV. PAUL JOHN, A.B., J.C.L., Attempted Marriages and Their Consequent Juridic Effects.
204. MUNDY, REV. THOMAS MAURICE, A.B., S.T.L., J.C.D., The Union of Parishes, X-164 pp., 1944.
205. O'DEA, REV. JOHN COYLE, A.B., J.C.D., The Matrimonial Impediment of Nonage, VIII-126 pp., 1944.
206. OLALIA, REV. ALEXANDER AYSON, S.T.L., J.C.D., A Comparative Study of the Christian Constitution of States and the Constitution of the Philippine Commonwealth, XII-136 pp., 1944.
207. POISSON, REV. PIERRE-MARIE, C.S.C., A.B., PH.L., TH.L., J.C.L., Droits Patrimoniaux des Maisons et des Eglises Religieuses.
208. STADALNIKAS, REV. CASIMIR JOSEPH, M.I.C., J.C.D., Reservation of Censures, X-141 pp., 1944.
209. SULLIVAN, REV. EUGENE HENRY, S.T.L., J.C.D., Proof of the Reception of the Sacraments, X-165 pp., 1944.
210. VAUGHAN, REV. WILLIAM EDWARD, J.C.D., Constitutions for Diocesan Courts, X-210 pp., 1944.
211. PARO, REV. GINO, S.T.D., J.C.D., The Right of Papal Legation, X-221 pp., 1944. (Printed, 1947).
212. BALZER, REV. RALPH FRANCIS, C.P., J.C.D., The Computation of Time in a Canonical Novitiate, X-227 pp., 1945.
213. DOUGHERTY, REV. JOHN WHELAN, A.B., S.T.L., J.C.D., De Inquisitione Speciali, XII-195 pp., 1945.
214. DZIOB, REV. MICHAEL WALTER, J.C.D., The Sacred Congregation for the Oriental Church, XII-181 pp., 1945.
215. EIDENSCHINK, REV. JOHN ALBERT, O.S.B., B.A., J.C.D., The Election of Bishops in the Letters of Pope Gregory the Great, VIII-200 pp., 1945.
216. GILL, REV. NICHOLAS, C.P., J.C.D., The Spiritual Prefect in Clerical Religious Houses of Study, X-140 pp., 1945.
217. HYNES, REV. HARRY GERARD, S.T.L., J.C.D., The Privileges of Cardinals, XII-183 pp., 1945.
218. MCDEVITT, REV. GERALD VINCENT, S.T.L., J.C.D., The Renunciation of an Ecclesiastical Office, XIV-179 pp., 1945.
219. MANNING, REV. JOSEPH LEROY, J.C.D., The Free Conferral of Offices, VII-116 pp., 1945.
220. MEYER, REV. LOUIS G., O.S.B., A.B., S.T.B., J.C.D., Alms-gathering by Religious, XII-163 pp., 1945.
221. O'DONNELL, REV. CLETUS FRANCIS, M.A., J.C.D., The Marriage of Minors, XII-268 pp., 1945.
222. PRUNSKIS, REV. JOSEPH, J.C.D., Comparative Law, Ecclesiastical and Civil, in Lithuanian Concordat, X-161 pp., 1945.
223. SWEENEY, REV. FRANCIS PATRICK, C.SS.R., J.C.D., The Reduction of Clerics to the Lay State, X-199 pp., 1945.
224. VOGELPOHL, REV. HENRY JOHN, J.C.D., The Simple Impediments to Holy Orders, XVI-190 pp., 1945.

225. BROCKHAUS, REV. THOMAS AQUINAS, O.S.B., J.C.D., Religious Who Are Known as *Conversi*, X-127 pp., 1945.
226. GRIESE, REV. ORVILLE NICHOLAS, S.T.D., J.C.D., Marriage and the Procreation of Offspring, XVI-224 pp., 1945.
227. BOUDREAUX, REV. WARREN LOUIS, J.C.D., The *"ab acatholicis nati"* of Canon 1099, § 2, XII-110 pp., 1946.
228. BOWE, REV. THOMAS JOSEPH, A.B., J.C.D., Religious Superioresses, VIII-206 pp., 1946.
229. DIEDERICHS, REV. MICHAEL FERDINAND, S.C.J., J.C.D., The Jurisdiction of the Latin Ordinaries over their Oriental Subjects, XIV-153 pp., 1946.
230. DINGMAN, REV. MAURICE JOHN, A.B., S.T.L., J.C.L., The Plaintiff in Contentious Trials.
231. FRISON, REV. BASIL, C.M.F., M.MUS., J.C.D., The Retroactivity of Law, X-221, pp. 1946.
232. GALVIN, REV. WILLIAM ANTHONY, M.A., J.C.D., The Administrative Transfer of Pastors, XII-288 pp., 1946.
233. GORACY, REV. JOSEPH C., J.C.L., The Diriment Matrimonial Impediment of Major Orders.
234. HALE, REV. JOSEPH FRANCIS, M.A., S.T.L., J.C.D., The Pastor of Burial, X-247 pp., 1946. (Printed, 1949).
235. HENRY, REV. JOSEPH ARTHUR, A.B., J.C.D., The Mass and Holy Communion: Interritual Law, XII-138 pp., 1946.
236. LINENBERGER, REV. HERBERT, C.PP.S., J.C.D., The False Denunciation of an Innocent Confessor, VIII-205 pp., 1946. (Printed, 1949).
237. LOWRY, REV. JAMES MARTIN, A.B., J.C.D., Dispensation from Private Vows, XII-216 pp., 1946.
238. LYNCH, REV. GEORGE EDWARD, A.B., S.T.L., J.C.D., Coadjutors and Auxiliaries of Bishops, X-107 pp., 1946. (Printed, 1947).
239. LYNCH, REV. TIMOTHY, M.S.SS.T., J.C.D., Contracts between Bishops and Religious Congregations, XIII-232 pp., 1946.
240. MCCLUNN, REV. JUSTIN DAVID, A.B., S.T.L., J.C.D., Administrative Recourse, VII-142 pp., 1946.
241. LOHMULLER, REV. MARTIN NICHOLAS, A.B., J.C.D., The Promulgation of Law, XII-140 pp., 1947.
242. MCGRATH, REV. JAMES, A.B., J.C.D., The Privilege of the Canon, XII-156 pp., 1946.
243. MARBACH, REV. JOSEPH FRANCIS, A.B., J.C.D., Marriage Legislation for the Catholics of the Oriental Rites in the United States and Canada, XIV-314 pp., 1946.
244. SHIMKUS, REV. BERNARD ALOYSIUS, A.B., J.C.L., The Determination and Transfer of Rite.
245. SMITH, REV. VINCENT MICHAEL, A.B., S.T.L., J.C.L., Ignorance Affecting Matrimonial Consent.
246. WACHTRLE, REV. PAUL ANTHONY, A.B., J.C.L., The Baptism of the Children of Non-Catholics.

247. CROTTY, REV. MATTHEW M., J.C.D., The Recipient of First Holy Communion, X-142 pp., 1947.
248. EAGLETON, REV. GEORGE, J.C.D., The Quinquennial Faculties, Formula IV, XIV-199 pp., 1947. (Printed, 1948).
249. GIBBONS, REV. MARION L., C.M., LL.B., J.C.D., Domicile of the Wife Unlawfully Separated from Her Husband, XIV-171 pp., 1947.
250. KELLY, REV. BERNARD M., S.T.L., J.C.D., The Functions Reserved to Pastors, IX-141 pp., 1947.
251. KILCULLEN, REV. THOMAS J., LL.M., J.C.D., The Collegiate Moral Person as Party Litigant, X-150 pp., 1947.
252. LAFONTAINE, REV. GERMAIN J., W.F., J.C.D., Relations Canoniques entre Le Missionnaire et Ses Superieurs, X-117 pp., 1947.
253. LANE, REV. LORAS T., A.B., S.T.L., J.C.D., Matrimonial Procedure in the Ordinary Court of Second Instance, XVI-184 pp., 1947.
254. LOVER, REV. JAMES F., C.SS.R., J.C.D., The Master of Novices, X-168 pp., 1947.
255. MCNICHOLAS, REV. TIMOTHY J., J.C.L., The *Septimae Manus* Witness.
256. MAROSITZ, REV. JOSEPH J., M.S.C., J.C.D., Obligations and Privileges of Religious Promoted to the Episcopal or Cardinalitial Dignities, XII-180 pp., 1947.
257. MURPHY, REV. FRANCIS J., A.B., J.C.D., Legislative Powers of the Provincial Council, XII-158 pp., 1947.
258. O'BRIEN, REV. ROMAEUS W., O.CARM., J.C.D., The Provincial Superior in Religious Orders of Men, X-294 pp., 1947.
259. PFALLER, REV. BENEDICT A., O.S.B., J.C.D., The *Ipso facto* Effected Dismissal of Religious, XII-225 pp., 1947.
260. POPEK, REV. ALPHONSE S., M.A., J.C.D., The Rights and Obligations of Metropolitans, XX-460 pp., 1947.
261. RISTUCCIA, REV. BERNARD J., C.M., J.C.D., Quasi-Religious, XVI-318 pp., 1947. (Printed, 1949).
262. SONNTAG, REV. NATHANIEL L., O.F.M.CAP., J.C.D., Censorship of Special Classes of Books, XII-147 pp., 1947.
263. STADLER, REV. JOSEPH N., J.C.D., Frequent Holy Communion, X-158 pp., 1947.
264. SZAL, REV. IGNATIUS J., J.C.D., The Communication of Catholics with Schismatics, XII-217 pp., 1947.
265. WAGNER, REV. URBAN S., O.F.M.CONV., J.C.D., Parochial Substitute Vicars and Supplying Priests, IX-126 pp., 1947.
266. QUINN, REV. JOSEPH, M.A., J.C.D., Documents Required for the Reception of Orders, XII-207 pp., 1948.
267. BENNINGTON, REV. JAMES CLEMENT, A.B., J.C.L., The Recipient of Confirmation.
268. BLAHER, REV. DAMIAN JOSEPH, O.F.M., A.B., J.C.L., The Ordinary Processes in Causes of Beatification and Canonization.
269. CLUNE, REV. ROBERT BELL, B.A., J.C.L., The Judicial Interrogation of the Parties.

270. COURTEMANCHE, REV. BASIL F., B.A., J.C.L., The Total Simulation of Matrimonial Consent.
271. DLOUHY, REV. MAUR JOHN, O.S.B., A.B., J.C.L., The Ordination of Exempt Religious.
272. DONOVAN, REV. JOHN THOMAS, PH.B., S.T.L., J.C.D., The Clerical Obligations of Canons 138 and 140, XII-209 pp., 1948.
273. FREKING, REV. FREDERICK W., A.B., S.T.B., J.C.L., The Canonical Installation of Pastors.
274. FULTON, REV. THOMAS B., J.C.L., Prenuptial Investigation.
275. GODLEY, REV. JAMES P., J.C.L., The Time and the Place for the Celebration of Mass.
276. KANE, REV. THOMAS A., A.B., B.S., J.C.D., The Jurisdiction of the Patriarchs of the Major Sees in Antiquity and in the Middle Ages, XII-111 pp., 1948. (Printed, 1949).
277. KENNEDY, REV. ANDREW A., J.C.L., The Annual Pastoral Report to the Local Ordinary.
278. KONRAD, REV. JOSEPH GEORGE, J.C.L., Transfer of Religious.
279. KRESS, REV. ALPHONSE, J.C.L., Contumacy in Ecclesiastical Trials.
280. MCCARTNEY, REV. MARCELLUS ANTHONY, O.F.M., M.A., J.C.L., Faculties of Regular Confessors.
281. MCCASLIN, REV. EDWARD PATRICK, M.A., S.T.L., J.C.L., The Division of Parishes.
282. MCELROY, REV. FRANCIS J., A.B., J.C.L., The Privileges of Bishops.
283. QUINN, REV. STEPHEN, M.S.SS.T., J.C.L., Relation between the Local Ordinary and Religious of Diocesan Approval.
284. SCHNEIDER, REV. EDELHARD LOUIS, A.D.S., M.A., J.C.D., The Status of Secularized Ex-Religious Clerics, X-155 pp., 1948.
285. THOMPSON, REV. CHESTER J., A.B., J.C.L., The Simple Removal from Office.
286. O'BRIEN, REV. KENNETH R., A.B., J.C.D., The Nature of Support of Diocesan Priests in the United States, XVI-162 pp., 1949.
287. METZ, REV. JOHN E., S.T.L., J.C.D., The Recording Judge in the Ecclesiastical Collegiate Tribunal, X-130 pp., 1949.
288. REINHARDT, REV. MARION J., S.T.L., J.C.L., The Rogatory Commission.
289. ORTEGA UHINK, REV. JUAN, S.J., J.C.L., *De Delicto Sollicitationis.*
290. CASEY, REV. JAMES V., J.C.L., A Study of Canon 2222, § 1.
291. ALLGEIER, REV. JOSEPH L., J.C.L., The Canonical Obligation of Preaching in Parish Churches.
292. CAHILL, REV. DANIEL R., J.C.L., The Custody of the Holy Eucharist.
293. CARR, REV. AIDAN, O.F.M.CONV., S.T.D., J.C.L., Vocation to the Priesthood: Its Canonical Concept.
294. KNOPKE, REV. ROCH F., O.F.M., J.C.L., Reverential Fear in Matrimonial Cases in Asiatic Countries: Rota Cases.
295. LAVELLE, REV. HOWARD D., J.C.L., The Obligation of Holding Sacred Missions in Parishes.

296. MICHELLS, REV.. ANTHONY B., J.C.L., The Constitutive Elements of Parishes.
297. NOONE, REV. JOHN, J.C.L., Nullity in Judicial Acts.
298. SHEEHAN, REV. DANIEL E., J.C.L., The Minister of Holy Communion.
299. STATKUS, REV. FRANCIS J., J.C.L., The Minister of the Last Sacraments.
300. COOK, REV. JOHN P., J.C.L., Ecclesiastical Communities and Their Ability to Induce Legal Customs.
301. FAZZALARO, REV. FRANCIS J., The Place for the Hearing of Confessions.
302. HANNAN, REV. PHILIP M., J.C.L., The Canonical Concept of *Congrua Sustentatio* for the Secular Clergy.
303. QUINN, REV. HUGH G., S.T.L., J.C.L., The Particular Penal Precept.
304. GALLAGHER, REV. JOHN F., J.C.L., The Matrimonial Impediment of Public Propriety.
305. WELSH, REV. THOMAS J., J.C.L., The Use of the Portable Altar.

www.ingramcontent.com/pod-product-compliance
Lightning Source LLC
LaVergne TN
LVHW050203080826
844660LV00012B/343
* 9 7 8 0 8 1 3 2 2 4 7 0 1 *